HIDDEN MYTH
STRUCTURE & SYMBOLISM IN ADVERTISING

Varda Langholz Leymore

HIDDEN MYTH

STRUCTURE & SYMBOLISM IN ADVERTISING

HEINEMANN
LONDON

Heinemann Educational Books Ltd

LONDON EDINBURGH MELBOURNE AUCKLAND TORONTO
HONG KONG SINGAPORE KUALA LUMPUR
IBADAN NAIROBI JOHANNESBURG
LUSAKA NEW DELHI

ISBN o 435 82518 6
© Varda Langholz Leymore 1975
First published 1975

Published by Heinemann Educational Books Ltd
48 Charles Street, London W1X 8AH
Printed and bound in Great Britain by
Morrison and Gibb Ltd, London and Edinburgh

Contents

Dedication

To Gideon

Acknowledgements

I would like to thank Professor D. G. MacRae, who supervised this study, and who initiated me in structuralism. His guidance and support throughout this work have been a source of constant inspiration. I would like, further, to thank Mr G. de Groot who gave me the benefit of his vast knowledge and his rich experience in advertising research. He also made available to me the samples of commercials which were used in this study. It is with a sense of gratitude and real joy that I acknowledge my indebtedness to my husband Gideon Langholz and the special contribution he made to this work. It was his wish that I should undertake it and it was his fortitude, persistence and resolution which sustained me during the long difficult months. His contribution was not only moral but also material. In particular his knowledge of mathematics and communications theory were instrumental in helping to formulate the methodological framework. Mr Sadarangani, Mr Dunn and Miss Tenné were extremely helpful in explaining to me some intricate statistical methods and in teaching me how to use a computer.

Introduction

Even the most familiar phenomena require explanation.
                                                    Chomsky

The genesis of this book is in curiosity. When the preliminary work was undertaken, structuralism was enjoying an unprecedented notoriety. Lévi-Strauss has just published his third volume of Mythologiques.[1] The first volume, *The Raw and the Cooked* appeared in an English translation and created a great deal of clamour. The second volume was on the translator's desk, awaited by an impatient public. In France raging debates between the Existentialists and the Structuralists dominated the social science scene.[2] A new subject, which was till then an obscure activity enjoyed by a dedicated minority, linguistics, came to the fore with relentless vigour. Old names such as de Saussure were revived and a new school under the intellectual and philosophical guidance of Chomsky has appeared.[3] If structural linguistics did not become a household word, Chomsky and Lévi-Strauss did. In England, Edmund Leach fascinated and entertained the public with his analysis of the Old Testament monarchs and the stories of Genesis.[4]

A new interdisciplinary or supradisciplinary approach became the promise of the day. Insights from sophisticated computer technology and linear algebra became new potent tools in the understanding of human communication.[5] The facility of language became central to the understanding of human thinking and the structure of the unconscious.[6] Things which previously were regarded as straightforward common sense became complex manifestations of a highly regulated, if unknown, sign system. Different spheres of life were exposed as sharing essentially the same common rules.

In this climate of renewal it was hard to resist the temptation

vii

to try to examine the extent to which the basic principles of structuralism could be applied to a highly sophisticated system of communication, namely to modern advertising. Advertising is a communication system par excellence. It is essentially concerned with the use of symbols to effect the exchange of values. As such, it is the focal point of the two most important communication processes in any society—the exchange of signs and the exchange of money, goods and services. Advertising uses the discourse of words and images to bring about the dialogue of values.

To examine the extent to which advertising yields to structuralism, I decided to look at two types of advertising: static and dynamic—magazine advertising and television advertising. The magazine advertisements included five product areas during a one-year period and the television commercials covered three products through a period of four years.

It very quickly became apparent that the basic principles of structuralist analysis, as advocated by Lévi-Strauss, needed to be adapted to this particular case.[7] And so the first stage was to define more closely the methodology of deciphering. Here, as in other examples where structuralism was attempted, the basic problem was to identify the relationships between the elements in the system. Again as in other cases, the major difficulty stemmed from the fact that each advertisement is a complete meaningful entity in itself. Structuralism breaks this complete meaningful harmony into its component parts in order to show that, viewed from a different angle, these component parts form new relationships, which convey the fundamental or basic message. For instance, the commercial 'Happiness is a cigar called Hamlet' has a certain meaning in itself. However, if all the cigar commercials were to be assembled together and decoded as one system, it could well be that this commercial would be cast in a completely different role. In this new role, it will be precisely like a piece in a jigsaw puzzle whose meaning is revealed only through its relation to other pieces. The other pieces in this puzzle are the other commercials for cigars.

The second major problem was to come to grips with the concept of system. To determine the true boundaries of what constitutes and what does not constitute a true advertising system turned out to be a stubborn obstacle. Eventually, the realization that all the advertisements of one brand do not constitute a legitimate or decipherable advertising system (in competitive cases), while all the advertisements of all the competitive brands do, provided me with the clue to the structures of the sub-systems, in the overall advertising system. Thereafter, the analysis was fairly straightforward, and its conclusions, if correct, rather striking. These are fully discussed in Chapters 6 and 7.

I would only comment here, that the final message received in the viewer's mind is based on the system *in toto* not on individual advertisements for any one brand, and certainly not on a single isolated advertisement. The message of a single representation will not get through unless it possesses a complete underlying structure. The discourse between advertisers and between advertiser and viewer is carried out not only on the well-recognized surface level, but also on the deep level. And finally, while neither is consciously aware of the reality or the existence of this other perception, it is nevertheless there.

Hitherto, the great majority of structural analyses were carried out on anthropological material, ancient legends and myths. My concern was with highly sophisticated modern advertising, which at least for all appearances bears little resemblance to the myths of the Bororo Indians, and is far removed from the stories of the Bible and even the Olympian Gods. Nevertheless, once decoded, they surrender very much the same systems of relationships and reveal the same fundamental rules of construction.

All societies modern and ancient, literate and illiterate, yield, once the key is found, the essential underlying unity of the symbolic function of the mind. The contents to which each society applies itself may be vastly different; but not the forms of thinking or the ability to think. That modern advertising is constructed like a tribal myth or Greek mythology, is but a small additional evidence of this profound unity.

Further, advertising performs in modern society much the same function that myth performs in other societies. As a myth in modern disguise it nevertheless has the same role as ancient myth. Lévi-Strauss defines this role to be the resolution of potential conflicts. Myths serve to reinforce accepted modes of behaviour by scanning all the alternative solutions and 'proving' that the one which predominates in any society, in given circumstances, is the best. As such, myth is precisely like advertising, a conservative force. It is not concerned with revolutionizing the

ix

existing order of things but in preserving it. Advertising advocates consumption of new products, or reinforces consumption of old products, but both are done using accepted themes and well-established symbols of happiness, health and success. Far from changing values, it very much follows and upholds existing ones. Over and beyond this, advertising (like myth) acts as an anxiety-reducing mechanism. This is done first by re-stating, on the deep level, the basic dilemmas of the human conditions; and second by offering a solution to them. It reiterates the essential problems of life—good and evil, life and death, happiness and misery, etc.—and simultaneously solves them. To the constant anxieties of life, advertising gives a simple answer. In consuming certain products, one buys not only a 'thing' but also an image. An image which invokes the belief and the hope of having the good rather than the bad, happiness rather than misery, success rather than failure, life rather than death. And the more anxious, confused, uncertain and bewildered modern society gets, the stronger will be the role played by advertising.

The first chapter is devoted to a brief summary of the main postulates of structuralism. Chapter 2 outlines the methodology used in this study. It is followed by two major demonstrations of the method of work: Chapter 3, which examines static advertising, and Chapter 4, which looks at dynamic advertising. Treading on a somewhat foreign ground in the context of this study, Chapter 5 presents an attempt to measure the efficacy of the Exhaustive Common Denominators in terms of their impact on the market. Chapter 6 deals with the major implications of the findings for advertising and pursues some relevant topics of particular interest. Finally, in Chapter 7, having completed a full circle, we return to the beginning to examine the implications of the findings from a broader structuralist point of view.

References

1. C. Lévi-Strauss, *Mythologiques* I, II, III, IV (Paris: Plon, 1964, 1966, 1968, 1971). *The Raw and the Cooked* (I) first appeared in English translation in 1970, and *From Honey to Ashes* (II) in 1972.
2. See for instance, C. Lévi-Strauss, *The Savage Mind* (Weidenfeld & Nicolson, 1966); Lévi-Strauss, *Structural Anthropology* (Allen Lane, 1968); A. J. Greimas, *Du Sens* (Paris: Editions du Seuil, 1970).
3. F. de Saussure, *Course in General Linguistics* (McGraw-Hill, 1966); N. Chomsky, *Language and Mind* (New York: Harcourt, Brace & World,

1968); E. H. Lennenberg, *Biological Foundations of Language* (New York: John Wiley, 1967).

4. E. Leach, *Genesis as Myth* (Jonathan Cape, 1969); Leach, *C. Lévi-Strauss* (Fontana, 1970); Leach, ed, *The Structural Study of Myth* (Tavistock Publications, 1967).

5. R. Boudon, *The Uses of Structuralism* (Heinemann, 1971); P. Maranda, 'The computer and the analysis of myth', in *International Social Science Journal*, vol. XXIII, No. 2 (1971), pp. 228–335.

6. J. Lacan, 'L'instance de la lettre dans l'inconscient ou la raison depuis Freud' (in English), Yale French Studies, *Structuralism*, pp. 112–47.

7. C. Lévi-Strauss, 'The structural analysis of myth' in *Structural Anthropology*; E. Leach, *Lévi-Strauss*; R. Barthes, *Elements of Semiology* (Jonathan Cape, 1967).

1. Structuralism—the protagonist introduced

Invention, it must be humbly admitted, does not consist in creating out of void but out of chaos. Mary Shelley

This study explores one fundamental question and its various ramifications. It is postulated at the outset, that *les images publicitaires* may be regarded as a system of signs. If this assumption is correct, it should be possible to demonstrate that the many representations of the advertising system are reducible to an underlying structure. The main part of this book is devoted to the examination of this single hypothesis, the nature of the underlying structure; and the various implications, both theoretical and practical, which stem from this point of view. Before turning, however, to the specific area which concerns us here, the main theoretical tools must be introduced.

As a new approach in the social sciences structuralism is, with the exception of linguistics and structural anthropology, still in its infancy. The basic concepts of structuralism are quite old. Yet a discussion of its impact as a new method for the human sciences normally refers to the way in which modern linguistic theory influences other disciplines within the social sciences.

The basic confusion in structuralism results, for some, in an ambiguity between the fundamental theoretical premises of the approach and its methodological perspective. Some scholars regard structuralism as merely a method which is designed to attack well-known problems by the use of specially adapted linguistic and quasi-algebraic tools. Others claim, taking almost the opposite view, that structuralism has developed into a full-fledged theory without, however, acknowledging this fact or working out its implications.[1]

I

The contention that structuralism fails to realize the consequences of its basic premises seems to me to be unwarranted; and the criticism concerning the priority of method, taken at its face value, is wrong by definition, for no method could exist in a theoretical vacuum. Yet this disconcerted feeling seems to reflect a general property of structuralism, a feeling that methodology enjoys a special status in this philosophy. Contrary to other theories, particularly in the social sciences, it is, as Roland Barthes claims in a remarkable passage, the method that makes the theory.[2] Structuralists, having embarked on a voyage destined to bring them to a land where order does not only reign (for it reigns everywhere) but also where it is seen to reign, have gradually realized that the navigation is not just an aid to transportation from one place to another but conceals in itself the promised land. From an activity mainly concerned with unveiling order in diverse, seemingly unconnected phenomena, it has grown into a realization of the existence of a new order of things, a realization with bold premises, which if confirmed (as this is only the beginning), will have a momentous effect on all the sciences of man.

I will look first at the linguistic foundations of structuralism, proceed to examine their implications and the theoretical speculations resulting from them, and then end with some general observations and qualifications. Structuralism is by no means a new concept. It has been applied in many guises, using more stringent methods or less stringent ones as the occasion demanded, in many fields of research ranging from mathematics to literary criticism. However, the full implications of the notion in the social sciences (economics excluded) have come to be recognized only fairly recently. The major influence in this respect was exerted by modern linguistic theory, which was then further enhanced and amplified by borrowing and applying some notions and techniques from information theory, cybernetics and modern algebra.

Linguistic theory has become, however, the exemplary model or, in a sense, the science in science. This once remote and esoteric activity is rapidly becoming a kernel of inspiration and a challenge to time-honoured dogma.[3] Thus, at least as far as some of the social sciences are concerned, the more thought-provoking contributions are associated with the new vistas opened by structuralism. Most renowned of these are of course works in structural anthropology with Lévi-Strauss as its most distinguished exponent.[4] Others, no less important, are Lacan's psychoanalysis,[5] Althusser's Marxism,[6] Foucault's philosophy,[7] Roland Barthes' semiology and literary criticism,[8] Greimas' semantics,[9] Piaget's psychology,[10] Propp's folktale studies,[11] and the list goes on. Sadly and somewhat surprisingly, sociology proper, with some notable exceptions, has been rather slow to succumb to the temptations of this new method.[12]

One may wonder, then, what it is in linguistic theory that created such a tremor and produced such a wealth of new insights. The European tradition relies heavily on de Saussure and his heritage; indeed the Saussurean notions which, when formulated some seventy years ago, were either partially or completely novel, still constitute with some modifications the foundations of the linguistically inspired approach in areas other than linguistics. Some well-known examples are Lévi-Strauss' kinship and myth studies as well as Barthes' fashion system.

The first of the now famous Saussurean distinctions is that between *langue* (language) and *parole* (speech). This distinction concerns the difference between a collective a priori given, a system of rules and word conventions, which is indifferent to the materials of the signals which compose it and is independent of any individual user—and the individual utilization of the language which consists basically of an act of selection, and the ordering of the selected elements, in accordance with the basic rules of the language.[13] This distinction is rather similar to the one drawn by Chomsky between the notions of competence and performance, where competence denotes the underlying system of regulations and language parts, and performance, the individual use of this system. An example may clarify these concepts: in the cinema, which is a semiological system, any specific film is the speech of that underlying system of cinema language, which is, according to Christian Metz, the ordered combinations of movement, musical signs, verbal signs and noise.[14] Incidentally, in semiological systems the distinction is not nearly as clear cut as it is in linguistic systems proper, but let us not enter into this debate now.

The second Saussurean insight concerns the distinction between the *signifier* and the *signified*. The signifier is that complex of

sounds which denotes a concept; the signified is quite simply
the concept thus evoked. Saussure carefully emphasizes that
the signifier is not 'the material sound, a purely physical thing,
but the psychological imprint of the sound, the impression that
it makes on our senses.'[15] The union of a signifier and a signified,
the collection of sounds forming a word and the mental
representation of this sound, make together the linguistic sign.
This linguistic sign is the combination which conveys an idea as
a whole.

Lacan, elaborating on this relation, to which Saussure was
prepared to give only a unique value, claims that in reality each
signifier may have different signifieds depending on the specific
context in which the sign occurs.[16] It is important to realize,
though, that in both interpretations the linguistic sign is capable
of conveying an idea specifically because it is made up of a sense
as well as a sound which signifies this sense, and because, in a
larger chain of speech, it has a prescribed position vis-à-vis the
other signs in the chain.

The signifying function of language leads to a third Saussurean
observation which concerns language as a system of differences
and oppositions. 'In language', says Saussure in a much quoted
epigraph, 'there are only differences.' A word is a unity of
differences, but the combination of two signs is a positive fact,
'two signs, each having a signified and a signifier, are not different
but only distinct. Between them there is only *opposition*. The
entire mechanism of language . . . is based on oppositions of this
kind and on the phonic and conceptual differences that they
imply.'[17] This system of oppositions is crucial for any transmission
of meaning. Meaning or, as de Saussure preferred to call it, the
value of a word, is not inherent in it but is external to it; indeed
an element in itself is meaningless because meaning is not a
property of unrelated elements but emanates rather from the
relationships between them. 'Language is a system of inter-
dependent terms in which the value of each term results solely
from the simultaneous presence of the others.'[18] In summary,
then, sense resides in the positional relationships of elements,
not in the elements themselves. This is by no means an uncontroversial matter even among structuralists. However, it
is a fundamental philosophical premise which stems directly
from the Saussurean position outlined above.

4

To the uninitiated, this is rather difficult to accept because of the very strong feeling that words such as 'cloud', 'moon' or 'table' do have some meaning in themselves, which does not necessarily stem from their relations to other words. It seems possible to bridge this apparent gulf between 'common sense' and the structuralist 'non-sense' by giving it an interpretation which is based upon information theory. If we equate information with meaning, it can be said that a word, expressed by itself, has minimal information content because it allows for a maximum choice.* By itself it does not disclose what 'it means' as we are free to choose any meaning from a wide range of possibilities. When a word appears in a context, e.g. a sentence or a collection of sentences, this context constrains the number of ways in which it might be understood. Hence, its information content, and therefore its meaning, increases. So if we just utter the word 'cloud' this may evoke a representation of a grey patch up there in the sky; in England, noticing a cloud may be followed by a sigh of regret because it almost certainly means another rainy day, while in a drought, a cloud is greeted with joy because it signals rain. Being a cloud does not mean the same thing in these two widely different contexts.

The idea of binary oppositions achieved general acclaim especially with the works of Jacobson and Halle, who showed that the complex systems of oppositions between phonemes in all languages may be classified in terms of a few features, which can be specified in absolute language-independent terms, and which are of a binary nature.[19] It is thus that the notion of binary opposition became a fundamental of universal grammar with far-reaching effects on the development of structuralism.[20]

The only disciplines where this concept is rigorously applicable, besides some aspects of linguistics, are logic and mathematics. Other sciences must introduce a measure of arbitrariness into their exploits. In logic, binary oppositions are any two mutually exclusive and exhaustive elements. These elements are of necessity

---

* It should be noted that in terms of conventional information theory, maximum (rather than minimum) information content is associated with maximum choice. My approach deviates from the convention since I associate minimum information with maximum choice. Clearly, this approach does not violate the underlying philosophy of information theory, it merely constitutes the other side of the same coin.

also complementary because, given the definition above, they form one universe of discourse. The two terms of a binary opposition will be denoted as a and $\bar{a}$ (not a). For example, if failure and success are the only two options, a probability of 0·8 of success (a) implies a probability of 0·2 of failure ($\bar{a}$). Failure and success are mutually exclusive, exhaustive and complementary and form one universe of discourse.

In the various adaptations of binarism in other spheres, though the basic concept remains unchanged, the application is more flexible simply because there are only few straightforward as and not as. Some pairs are more sharply defined than others. Life can be safely assumed to be the opposite of death, but mother, for instance, may be claimed to be the binary opposition of father. Yet, one could argue with equal vigour that mother is, in fact, the binary opposition of daughter. The closest sense in which binary pairs may be used here in comparison with logic or mathematics are in such pairs as male/female or married/single, where the criterion is that the denial of one implies the unequivocal assertion of the other. In such cases, one of the two elements that constitute the binary opposition is redundant; for example, 'male' and 'not male' can represent the male/female pair. This is in sharp contrast to, for example, 'not father' which does not necessarily imply 'mother' or any other unique converse term. There are, then, some but not too many pure logical binary oppositions. Yet we are concerned with symbolic perception and though logics may rule out certain binary pairs as being inaccurate (a fact which gave rise to heated controversies) it is perfectly feasible to assume that within the boundaries of certain specific human contexts, such pairs are *perceived* as opposites. This is, as will become clearer later, a key assumption of this study.

The elements forming the binary pairs are analogous to phonemes, and depending on the system in question, they may be kinship terms, mythemes, clothing parts, furniture pieces and so on. They are normally referred to as constituent units or elementary segments. The identification of the relevant units constitutes the first step of any structuralist analysis.

The binary approach produced a long series of exciting studies.[21] Recently, however, some reservations have been expressed for two quite different reasons. In the first place it is claimed that, although

6

some parts of human perception can undoubtedly be explained in this way, it is by no means clear that all human thought is as a rule dichotomized in this fashion. Moreover, the structures of pattern recognition and pattern generation obey much more intricate and complex rules than is implied by the simple notion of binary oppositions.[22] Secondly, this model, like a digital computer, is two-valued, i.e. capable of 'yes' and 'no' or 'true' and 'false' answers, and does not allow for the possibility of admitting different grades of the same implicit dimension. There is no sensible way of conceiving, say, the 'sky' as gradually, bit by bit, turning into 'earth'. In this sense they do not lie on the same continuum and may be regarded as two logical binary oppositions. However, there is also comparative opposition in the sense in which one talks about something being more or less than something else. For instance, 'beautiful' is usually conceived as being the opposite of 'ugly' (digital computer model), but what about 'more beautiful'? Clearly, 'more beautiful' implies that something else is less beautiful though not necessarily 'ugly'. This type of gradable opposition is extremely widespread and consequently there is a definite case for invoking an analogue as well as a digital computer model. The difficulties inherent in such an approach arise from the fact that, at times, values which can only be understood as gradable opposites in this sense, acquire contrasting qualities which are felt to be absolute; a classical example of this is good and evil. Yet, in all cases such as this, the sense of opposition always stems from the fact that the terms are discussed with respect to some implicit norm.[23]

There are, then, at least three possible different types of oppositions that can be classified as follows:

(a) Binary oppositions in the same sense as in logic, e.g. male/not-male, where 'not-male' is inevitably 'female'.

(b) Oppositions with comparative grading on the same implicit dimension, e.g. good/bad where 'not good' is not necessarily 'bad' and vice versa.

(c) Oppositions whose elements are mutually exclusive as in (a), but not gradable as in (b), and which do not form the universe of discourse as in both (a) and (b), e.g. sun/moon. The elements of these pairs are conceived as being in some sense converse to each other.

7

This classification will be more rigorously examined in Chapter 2.

I would not have devoted this rather lengthy discussion to the binary question, were it not for the fact that a clear understanding of the problems involved is essential for any structuralist analysis. Many discussions concerning the validity of certain findings could have been avoided if the concepts were clearly defined in the first place. But let me return to de Saussure.

The whole idea of structuralism is founded on the *synchronic* orientation, which freezes a system in one moment of time only to revive it again in such a way as to obtain a total description of its operation and internal relationships as a closed whole. *Diachronic* studies, on the other hand, trace the development of a system, or parts of a system, through time. Thus, while the synchronic orientation puts at the centre of investigation a closed system of relationships, a diachronic orientation emphasizes the changes that elements of the system undergo. In principle, any diachronic axis can be broken down into synchronic stages. The major difficulty here is to determine for each communication system what span of time constitutes a synchronic unit. This is by no means a simple problem. When Roland Barthes, for instance, wishes to study fashion he assures us that it changes by a decree of the designers' élite once a year, and therefore each fashion year constitutes a single synchronic system. However, other cases—cinema, advertising, novels, etc.—do not lend themselves so easily to a rigid synchronic determination and thus what constitutes a change *of* the system (or some of its details) and what constitutes a change *in* the system may prove to be a stringent problem.

Finally, it was de Saussure who distinguished between syntagmatic and paradigmatic relations, though the modern conception of the latter has changed considerably. Syntagmatic relations are quite simply the permissible ways in which elements succeed each other in a chain of discourse. These elements have nothing in common and they are brought together by virtue of syntactic rules. Paradigmatic relations are those which belong to the same set by virtue of a function they share, in the sense that they occupy the same position in a chain of discourse. Thus, a sign enters into *paradigmatic* relations with all the signs which can also occur in the same context but not at the same time. The same sign enters into *syntagmatic* relations with other signs of

8

the same level with which it simultaneously occurs and which constitutes its context.[24]

Extending these notions beyond linguistics into other semiological systems, Jacobson has shown that metaphors belong to the paradigmatic order and metonymy to the syntagmatic order. This is recognized as an important breakthrough because it points to the way in which semiology could use linguistic insights in non-linguistic systems. An example given by Barthes may clarify this matter.[25] In the garment system, the paradigmatic order is illustrated by a 'set of pieces, parts or details which cannot be worn at the same time on the same part of the body, and whose variation corresponds to a change in the meaning of the clothing: toque-bonnet-hood etc.' The syntagmatic order is the 'juxtaposition in the same type of dress of different elements: skirt-blouse-jacket.'

One may go on exploring the linguistic 'foundations' of structuralism almost indefinitely. However, I shall stop here to consider some of their implications. Following the notions of meaning as emanating from relations between elements that are in themselves meaningless, structuralism puts the emphasis on totalities, and logical priority is given to the relations making up the whole over the parts and over the relations among the parts. Indeed, it is a fundamental premise that human phenomena can only be understood in terms of law-abiding relations between parts and wholes. Insisting upon *l'attitude totalisante* is a direct consequence of the linguistic principles outlined above.

Following linguistics, structuralism seeks the laws of formation not on the surface at the level of the observed, but somewhere behind or beneath it. The road to the truth is blocked by 'conscious models' which stand as a wall between the observer and the real appreciation of the organization of things; 'the more obvious structural organisation is, the more difficult it becomes to reach it because of the inaccurate conscious models lying across the path which leads to it.'[26] It is like a man who cannot see the landscape because he is giving his full attention and focusing his power of observation on the glass of the window.[27]

The analogy between this hidden structure and the notion of language, and between the surface structure and speech is clear. Just as in language any native speaker constantly applies the phonological and grammatical rules of his language without

9

being consciously aware of the existence of such rules, or, for that matter, that he is using them—so in other spheres of human endeavour certain unconscious laws, certain structuring principles are at the root of all systematic behaviour. Individual behaviour is constrained to choose from this underlying base and to abide by its rules. Lévi-Strauss in a beautiful passage sums up this argument.

> Linguistics thus presents us with a dialectical and totalising entity but one outside (or beneath) consciousness and will. Language, an unreflecting totalisation, is human reason which has its reasons and of which man knows nothing. And if it is objected that it is so only for a subject who internalises it on the basis of linguistic theory, my reply is that this way out must be refused, for this subject is one who *speaks*: for the same light which reveals the nature of language to him also reveals to him that it was so when he did not know it, for he already made himself understood, and that it will remain so tomorrow without his being aware of it, since his discourse never was and never will be the result of a conscious totalisation of linguistic laws.[28]

The secrets of the mind are many. For Chomsky, whatever happens there in the mind is responsible for the most fascinating quality of language, its unceasing creativity, tireless productivity. Because of this faculty of language Chomsky named his theory generative grammar. This is not all. The structuring ability of the mind is not acquired, but is there; it therefore must be innate, an attribute which is species specific. *L'esprit humain* is determined by internal constraints, an initial schemata which is generic and categorical and which predisposes a member of the human species to acquire certain modes of behaviour which hitherto (at least in the last two hundred and odd years) were considered to be in some sense cultural or learnt.[29]

Thus by imposing a form which in itself is finite and restrictive on limitless contents, the whole diversity of human activity may be accounted for and explained. Man has very often had 'recourse to the same means for solving problems whose concrete elements may be very different but which share the feature of all belonging to "structures of contradictions".'[30] This leads us to a further insight: the essential activity of the human mind is classificatory and its most fundamental rules may be reduced to those of contradictions and permutations—in other words, to binary oppositions. 'When the classificatory intention ascends, as it were, towards the greatest generality and most extreme abstraction, no diversity prevents it from applying a scheme through the operation of which reality undergoes a series of progressive purifications,whose final term will be provided, as intended in the form of a simple binary opposition.'[31] Thus the innate structuring ability of the human mind can be expressed in the form of binary oppositions and, consequently, the binary oppositions with the highest generalizing force are, in the last resort, the invariants or the universals of the human mind. It is important to realize that their universality is not inherent in them, but reflects the structuring activity of the mind.

If all human activity is simultaneously generated and constrained by the unconscious activity of the mind which has only one structure, then it is only logical to assume that the various more specialized 'micro' structures of which we may become conscious, are in fact various realizations of the same fundamental principles. It follows that the unconscious structure of the mind manifests itself in all types of human activity and therefore ultimately they can all be understood in terms of this all powerful and all encompassing structure: '*Au sens structuraliste, l'essentiel est que la structure peut être retrouvée dans différents ensembles. Une structure, au sens structuraliste, est la loi de formation et d'intelligibilité de divers ensembles.*'[32] It is in this sense that Lévi-Strauss' notion of the 'order of orders' must be understood. It is on the one hand the summary expression of a whole which is composed of sub-wholes; and permits, on the other hand, the comparison and association of all structures on all levels. 'The *order of orders* is not a mere logical reformulation of phenomena which have been subjected to analysis. It is the most abstract expression of the inter-relationships between the levels to which structural analysis can be applied, general enough to account for the fact that the models must sometimes be the same for societies which are historically and geographically disparate.'[33]

If the innate structuring of the mind is one, and if human manifestations may be deciphered in terms of their homologous codes, one is inexorably led to one inevitable conclusion—that, at the very least, symbolic perception and human thought follow the same laws everywhere. Thus: the binary oppositions, which are at one and the same time the most abstract and the simplest expression of human thought, are also the invariant universal forms of the human mind. As they go about the essentially classificatory activity of the mind they tirelessly demonstrate an activity which is essentially the same everywhere.

One problem is still left unanswered: how is the deep structure realized in the observed behaviour of man? The Chomskean answer to this is, in short, through transformation rules. It will be realized in the following example that the sense in which the term deep structure is used by Chomsky is somewhat different from the previous understanding, which identified it with the unconscious structuring rules of the mind. The resemblance is clear. The Chomskean deep structure is in the mind and is unconscious. The difference is in the level of specificity and rigorosity in which the concept is applied. In other words, though the deep structure is always an unconscious principle of the mind, different groups of sentences of similar characteristics, will each have their own independent deep structure. This basically means that it is the deep structure which gives the sentence its meaning, and it is the diversity of deep structures which, in ambiguous sentences, endows the same surface structure with different meanings. To illustrate this, let us turn to an example given by Chomsky.[34] The sentence 'a wise man is honest' has the following deep structure:

(1)

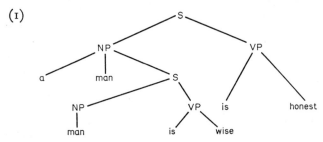

where S denotes sentence, NP noun phrase, and VP verb phrase. The surface structure of the same sentence is:

(2)

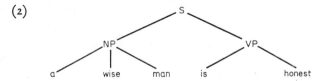

In the present case the surface structure can be formed from the deep structure by using the following transformation rules:

(*a*) Assign the marker *wh* to the most deeply embedded NP, 'man'
(*b*) Replace the NP so marked by 'who'
(*c*) Delete 'who is'
(*d*) Invert 'man' and 'wise'.

'Applying just operations (*a*) and (*b*) we derive the structure underlying the sentence "a man who is wise is honest", which is one possible realization of the underlying structure (1). If, furthermore, we apply the operation (*c*) (deriving 'a man wise is honest') we must, in English, also apply the subsidiary operation (*d*), deriving the surface structure (2).'[35]

Thus, the rules of transformation in the Chomskean scheme are the laws which relate the deep structure to the surface structure. It will be realized that in principle this concept is similar to the one adopted in social anthropology, and which denotes law-like regularities by which one particular cultural configuration changes into another.[36] The point which distinguishes, however, the latter concept from the previous one is that the transformation takes place between two equal homologous systems, and not between two different strata of the same system: the deep structure and its surface realization. Thus, in society 'similar properties are rediscovered in systems which are apparently different.'[37] If one assumes, as Lévi-Strauss does, that systems are ruled by codes, then by breaking these codes it is possible to transpose one system into another. This goes back to the idea elaborated above that social activity is built up of homologous structures. 'In a *different order of reality*', says Lévi-Strauss, 'kinship phenomena are phenomena of the *same type* as linguistic ones.'[38]

At this point a certain confusion becomes apparent between two key terms: structure and transformation. From one point of view, as in Chomsky's example above, the deep structure, the surface structure and the transformation rules that relate them to each other are quite distinct. This may be presented as in the following diagram.

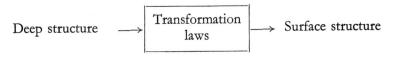

Deep structure ⟶ | Transformation laws | ⟶ Surface structure

However, this separation is arbitrary and analytic, for both the deep structure and the transformations exist in the mind only. From another point of view, the dynamics of the deep structure are in fact that of the transformation laws. As Piaget declares: 'if the character of structured wholes depends on their laws of composition, these laws must of their very nature be structuring: it is the constant duality, or bipolarity, of always being simultaneously *structuring* and *structured* that accounts for the success of the notion of law or rule employed by structuralists.'[39] To put it more concisely *the transformation is the structure*. To clarify this I must go back to the beginning.

Structuralism strives to build up a model which explains how the human mind works. More specifically, the human mind is viewed as an intermediary tool which receives signals from its environment, processes them in accordance with some rules which are 'programmed' into it, and which are called the deep structure, and then reproduces them in the various communication systems we have. In terms of structuralist theory, the mind receives a code and deciphers it to reveal its message. However, if this is correct, then the mind itself is the prototypical structure, i.e. a set of constraining rules, on which all other structures are modelled. The systems which it generates can never be the unique deep structure (no more than one could produce in this fashion the unconscious), but the more specialized structures of human activity which are homologous with the structure of the mind. This may be presented as in the following diagram.

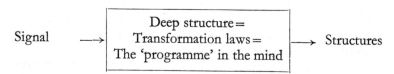

$$\text{Signal} \longrightarrow \boxed{\begin{array}{c} \text{Deep structure} = \\ \text{Transformation laws} = \\ \text{The 'programme' in the mind} \end{array}} \longrightarrow \text{Structures}$$

I suggest, therefore, that the deep structure in this sense is always in the mind and thus identical with the laws of transformation which govern its operation.

Despite the terminological confusion the 'two models' are in fact one. If we recall that in the first model above (page 13), both the deep structure and the transformations occur in the mind, then in terms of the second model they properly belong in the 'central box'. One is left in the first model with an unfinished system which consists of a 'white box' and an output. This 'crippled' system can be completed if we agree that the real input into that model are meaningless signs such as sounds, light waves and so on.

The ambitious pursuit of structuralism is to 'fill up' the Lockean 'empty cabinet', i.e. to explain the hidden work of the 'black box' and render it transparent. In other words to find its structure.

I may perhaps conclude this section with a reservation. Semiological studies derive a great inspiration from linguistics, yet in most cases they fall short of complying with probably its most revolutionary aspect, the infinite creativity of the base rules. In most semiological studies the identification of structure is tantamount to creating formal schemata into which all individual members of the system may, following some rules, be reduced. However, the converse is not true. The systems are incapable of generating one single example which belongs to their universe of discourse, in the sense that Chomsky is able to generate sentences. In other words, the rules enabling one to 'transform back' from the deep structure to the surface structure, are not specified. In this sense most semiological studies are not generative but static. I look more deeply into these questions in the next chapter.

References

1. See, for example, M. Lane, ed., *Structuralism* (Jonathan Cape, 1970), p. 18; D. M. Schneider, 'Some muddles in the models' in M. Banton, ed., *The Relevance of Models for Social Anthropology* (Tavistock Publications, 1965); H. G. Nutini, 'Some considerations on the nature of social structure and model building' in E. N. Hayes and T. Hayes, eds, *Claude Lévi-Strauss* (M.I.T. Press, 1970).

2. R. Barthes, 'L'activité structuraliste' in *Essais critiques* (Paris: Editions du Seuil, 1964), p. 216.

3. A few examples will suffice here: C. Lévi-Strauss, *Totemism* (Penguin Books, 1969); Lévi-Strauss, *Mythologiques*, I, II, III, IV (Paris: Plon, 1964, 1966, 1968, 1971); N. Chomsky, 'A review of B. F. Skinner's *Verbal Behaviour*' in J. A. Fodor and J. J. Katz, *The Structure of Language* (New Jersey: Prentice-Hall, 1964), pp. 547-78.

4. See, for example, C. Lévi-Strauss, *Totemism* and *Mythologiques*; Lévi-Strauss, *The Savage Mind* (Weidenfeld & Nicolson, 1966); Lévi-Strauss, *Structural Anthropology* (Allen Lane, 1968); Lévi-Strauss, *The Elementary Structures of Kinship* (Eyre & Spottiswoode, 1969).

5. J. Lacan, 'La causalité psychique' in *Evolution psychiatrique* fasc. I (1947); Lacan, 'Les formations de l'inconscient', Seminar 1958–59, *Bulletin de Psychologie*; Lacan, 'Fonction et champs de la parole et du langage en

psychanalyse', *Ecrits* (1966), pp. 237–322; Lacan, 'L'instance de la lettre dans l'inconscient ou la raison depuis Freud', ibid, pp. 493–528.

6. L. Althusser, *Pour Marx* (Paris: Maspero, 1965); Althusser with others, *Lire le Capital*, 2 vols (Paris: Maspero, 1965).

7. M. Foucault, *L'Archéologie du savoir* (Paris: Gallimard, 1969); Foucault, *Les mots et les choses* (Paris: Gallimard, 1966).

8. R. Barthes, *Essais critiques*, op. cit.; Barthes, *Elements of Semiology* (Jonathan Cape, 1967); Barthes, *Système de la Mode* (Paris: Editions du Seuil, 1967).

9. A. J. Greimas, *Du sens* (Paris: Editions du Seuil, 1970).

10. Jean Piaget, *The Origins of Intelligence in Children* (New York: Norton, 1963); Piaget, *The Mechanism of Perception* (New York: Basic Books, 1969); Piaget, *Biologie et Connaissance* (Paris: Gallimard, 1967); Piaget, *Genetic Epistemology*, Columbia University, Woodbridge Lectures no. 84, 1970; Piaget, *The Child's Conception of Time* (Routledge & Kegan Paul, 1969).

11. V. Propp, *Morphology of the Folktale* (Philadelphia: American Folklore Society, 1958).

12. Some sociological examples inspired by structuralism are P. K. Book, 'Social structure and language structure' in J. A. Fishman, ed., *Readings in the Sociology of Language* (The Hague: Mouton, 1970); B. Bernstein, 'Language in social strata and sectors', ibid.; Bernstein, 'Social class, linguistic codes and grammatical elements' in E. Keach, Jr. et al., *Education and Social Crises* (Wiley, 1967), pp. 221–40; Bernstein, 'On the classification and framing of educational knowledge' in M. Young, ed., *Knowledge and Control* (Collier-MacMillan, 1971). See also, B. Bernstein, *Class, Codes and Control*, vol. I, II and III (Routledge & Kegan Paul, 1971, 1973).

13. See, for example, R. Barthes, *Elements of Semiology*; E. Leach, *Lévi-Strauss* (Fontana, 1970); F. de Saussure, *Course in General Linguistics* (McGraw-Hill, 1966), pp. 13–20.

14. Taken from C. Metz, 'Propositions méthodologiques pour l'analyse du film', *Information sur les Sciences Sociales*, vol. 7, No. 4 (August, 1968), p. 108.

15. See F. de Saussure, op. cit., p. 66.

16. J. M. Auzias, *Clefs pour le structuralisme* (Paris: Seghers, 1971), pp 169–70.

17. F. de Saussure, op. cit., pp. 120–1.

18. Ibid., p. 114.

19. E. Leach, op. cit., pp. 28–30; also Leach, *Genesis as a Myth* (Cape Editions, 1969).

20. An excellent example of this is given by E. Leach, ibid.

21. E. Leach, *Lévi-Strauss* and *Genesis as a Myth*; also Leach, 'Animal categories and verbal abuse' in J. H. Greenberg, ed., *Universals of Language* (M.I.T. Press, 1963) and Introduction to *The Structural Study of Myth and Totemism*, A.S.A. Monograph 5 (Tavistock Publications, 1967). A. J. Greimas, 'La mythologie comparée' and 'Pour une théorie de l'interpretation du récit mythique' in *Du sens*, pp. 117–34 and 185–230; C. Lévi-Strauss, see reference 4; R. Barthes, see reference 8.

22. For example, E. Leach, *Lévi-Strauss*, pp. 112–13; Leach, 'Brain twister' in E. N. Hayes and T. Hayes, eds, *Claude Lévi-Strauss* (M.I.T. Press, 1970), pp. 128–30.
23. J. Lyons, *Introduction to Theoretical Linguistics* (Cambridge University Press, 1968), pp. 460–6.
24. Ibid., p. 73.
25. R. Barthes, *Elements of Semiology*, p. 63.
26. C. Lévi-Strauss, *Structural Anthropology*, p. 281.
27. From R. Barthes, *Le mythe, aujourd'hui*, quoted in J. Lawrence book review, *The Human Context* (August, 1968) (The Hague: Martinus Nijhoff), p. 114.
28. C. Lévi-Strauss, *The Savage Mind*, p. 252.
29. See, for example, N. Chomsky, op. cit.
30. C. Lévi-Strauss, *The Savage Mind*, p. 95.
31. Ibid., p. 217.
32. J. M. Auzias, op. cit., p. 13.
33. C. Lévi-Strauss, *Structural Anthropology*, p. 333.
34. N. Chomsky, *Language and Mind* (New York: Harcourt, Brace & World, 1968), pp. 25–6. Also J. P. B. Allen and P. van Buren, eds, *Chomsky: Selected Essays* (Oxford University Press, 1971), pp. 24–5.
35. N. Chomsky, *Language and Mind*, p. 26.
36. M. Lane, op. cit., p. 17.
37. C. Lévi-Strauss, 'Leçon Inaugurale', quoted in O. Paz, *Claude Lévi-Strauss* (Jonathan Cape, 1971), p. 12.
38. Quoted in O. Paz, ibid., p. 15.
39. J. Piaget, *Structuralism* (Routledge & Kegan Paul, 1971), p. 10.

2. A spade to dig with

The game is simply the totality of the rules which describe it.
J. Von Neumann

My approach to the study of advertising can best be understood as a process of transformation. This transformation involves the way in which signs or symbols are translated into real life action— the communication process through which advertising (the use of symbols) comes to influence the exchange of values (money, goods and services). Any purchasing behaviour which can be shown to be induced by advertising serves as an excellent illustration of the particularly thorny problem in communication, namely communication effectiveness. Needless to say, advertising is not the only factor at work in consumer markets, and consequently, the final outcome cannot be wholly attributed to it.

The very fact that advertising is viewed as a transformation process, which on the one hand encompasses the abstract influences, and on the other hand carries within itself the seeds of action, demands a type of analysis which is designed to reveal something about the message advertising conveys to the consumer. This study, therefore, is not an attempt to follow in the footsteps of the grammatic-semiologists, an endeavour in which the French both exult and excel, though, no doubt, some ideas raised by them influenced my way of thinking.[1]

Numerous studies, both commercial and academic, have been carried out in an attempt to unveil some of the mysteries of the persuasion process. Some of the most striking ideas were raised in Festinger's theory of cognitive dissonance, Katz's two steps flow of communication, Riesman's inner and other directedness, Roger's typology of adopters, Rokeach's classification of attitudes and values, Marshal McLuhan's celebrated ideas,[2] as well as those of others whose interests lay elsewhere, yet whose insights could provide important clues to this question. I will mention in this category just a few prominent names: Weber's theory of the Protestant ethic and capitalism, Sorokin's cultural mobility, Veblen's theory of the leisure class, Goffman's symbolic interactionism and Smelser's collective behaviour.[3] While the temptation to pursue these clues is considerable, it was felt that to start from a different theoretical platform could in the end prove more rewarding, and so I turned to structuralism. Within the boundaries of this theory, the focus of my interest is not, as was emphasized before, a formal image classification, but the understanding of the message.

There is another factor which influenced this decision. The existing number of semiological studies in this field of study is rather limited.[4] These are predominantly concerned with the reduction of phenomena under study into a formal schema, by whose defining features every visual image belonging to the system could be classified (e.g. cartoons, films, advertising, etc.).[5] Naturally, by adhering to this rigid grid, semiological studies are much closer to linguistics proper than any other branch of symbolic research. However, in my view, even though the semiological research is clearly exhaustive, classificatory and combinatory, it is not explicatory. Every signal may be properly classified but what it signifies remains a mystery. In contrast, I am concerned with adapting the insights of structuralism to my material with an interpretative object in mind, and in a way which is mostly inspired by Leach, Greimas and Lévi-Strauss.

Having put into perspective the framework within which I wish to work, one now can outline the characteristics of a structuralist model. There are a number of closely related ideas at work here. First, all parts of the model are interrelated in regularized ways. In this context, it is important to point out the fundamental difference, agreed upon by all structuralists, between structures and aggregates. With structures the emphasis is always on *wholes*, while aggregates are composed of elements which have an independent existence outside the system. Of course, structures are composed of elements too. However, 'the laws governing a structure's composition are not reducible to cumulative one-by-one association of its elements: they confer on the whole as such over-all properties distinct from the

properties of its elements'.[6] The model must include all the facts
that belong to and form the system, and not merely those which
seem to be 'important', a feeling which usually reflects some
theoretical or ideological preconception.

Second, since the system or the structured whole is formed
and defined in terms of the laws of composition, these laws
must be structuring. Hence, the system is both structured and
structuring, where the structuring aspects are, in my terminology,
the laws of transformation. By virtue of saying that a structure
is an ordered whole, this duality of structured-structuring can
be rephrased by introducing the notion that a transformation
is a structure and a structure is a transformation. Furthermore,
the transformations represent, or are in fact, the dynamic aspect
of the system. For a given system, it should be possible to
devise a variety of transformations which will result in a group
of homologous models.[7] Hence, it should be possible to predict
how a model will react if some of its elements undergo changes.[8]

Third, the system must be self-regulating which implies
self-maintenance and closure. In other words, the system must
perpetuate itself, and if elements are generated, they both belong
to the system and comply with its rules. Thus, generative
grammar, for example, has an infinite creative capacity; yet all
elements generated by it belong to it (closure), and the boundaries
of the structure are left unchanged (self-maintenance). Or, to
take another example, consider the system of decimal integers
under the operation of addition. The addition of any two integers
results in a third integer which belongs to the system. Lévi-
Strauss sums up the requirements of a structuralist model by the
principles that such a model must demonstrate 'economy of
explanation, unity of solution, and the ability to reconstruct the
whole from a fragment as well as later stages from previous
ones.'[9]

Searching the literature for a synthesized statement of a
technique, I came across a baffling number of directives. The
elements of faith and excitement, ambiguity and sweeping
generalizations on the one hand, and the computer-like precision
on the other hand make the reading fascinating but far from clear.
Some practical questions are also left without any clear answer.
The student may be puzzled about some such questions as: how
are the boundaries of the legitimate system of analysis determined?;

how does one 'reach' the underlying structure, assuming that it is there? And finally, a question which is of immediate concern to the topic at hand: what sort of structural analysis should be employed on advertisements? One may well imagine, that advertisements will yield to a Roland Barthes type of analysis, however, whether it is likely to yield also to a Lévi-Strauss or Edmund Leach kind of approach was rather less certain.

A partial encouragement is offered by the wide range of subjects handled by the structural method, though not all are handled with equal success. One feels, for instance, that the treatment of the Bororo myths is much more convincing than the analysis of the Oedipus myth. Whether the reason for this is the wider scope and extensive analysis of the first, or the better knowledge one has of the second is still being debated. Nevertheless, the topics do range from linguistics, where it all started, to literary criticism, to kinship systems, to myths, to riddles, to fairy tales and legends, to poetry, to modern thrillers, to mathematics, to philosophy and to fashion. One almost gets the impression that under the wide umbrella of structural analysis each field of investigation gives birth to the type of analysis best suited to it. Indeed there is no such thing as a standard structural analysis (apart perhaps from structural liguistics) but any analysis is structural if it complies with certain rules. I have attempted to reconstruct an operational tool of analysis from these fragments.

Following linguistics, structuralist analysis begins by breaking down the chain of discourse into the relevant minimal constituent units. This is rather similar to the procedure by which one identifies phonemes, mythemes or, for that matter, any other elementary segment on the level of specifity which is considered to be correct for the problem at hand. Having broken down the syntagmatic chains in this way, the constituent units can then be grouped into paradigmatic classes. We may recall that a syntagmatic chain is the permissible succession of elements in a universe of discourse, and paradigmatic groups are composed of elements which belong to the same class, by virtue of a function they share, and that they cannot simultaneously appear in the same context. Thus, it is impossible, for example, to advertise in the same copy two competing products. However, the advertisements for these products may enter into paradigmatic relations with each other. The paradigmatic classes may then be related to one another by a law of association. If this operation is successful, it may be concluded that the behaviour of the system is constrained by certain laws and that all its manifestations may be classified using a limited, finite number of rules.

In theory this may sound simple enough. In practice, however, the problems it presents are rather complex. I do not wish to pretend to have fully mastered semiological theory. Regrettably, I have not. What I intend to do is to try to apply to this problem some concepts and an approach adopted from structural anthropology, preferring as a rule the simpler solution to the complex one, and at times, when problems become really stringent, letting my imagination roam freely in the search for an answer. Let me first describe in some detail the technique I propose to use to analyse advertisements from a structuralist point of view.

According to Boudon,[10] any structuralist investigation which is designed to analyse a system, S, must have the following elements:

(a) A—a set of axioms which postulate a theory;
(b) $App (S)$—the apparent characteristics of the system, S;
(c) $Str (S)$—the structure of the system, S.
(d) A 'calculation' in terms of which either (a) and (b) are related to (c) or (a) and (c) are related to (b).

The form by which the axioms, the structure and the apparent characteristics are related to each other depends on the specific problem at hand. However, it may be summed up by the following two expressions:

$$\text{(I)} \quad A + Str (S) \xrightarrow{\text{calculation}} App (S)$$

$$\text{(II)} \quad A + App (S) \xrightarrow{\text{calculation}} Str (S).$$

The correct choice of expression depends on the nature of the problem. For instance, when the axioms and the structure are both given, as in Chomsky's theory of stress, the apparent characteristics of the system are the object of study, e.g., normal speech. In this context, it should be pointed out that the *App* (*S*) are independent of what the system itself is.[11] In view of my general frame of reference, the first formula may be conceived of as describing an *encoding* process.

My problem, though, is of a different nature. I seek to establish whether a structure may be deduced, assuming that the *App* (*S*) and the axioms are known. That is, the type of problem for which this study seeks an answer resides within the description of expression (II). The given element in this case are the apparent characteristics. The two other elements—the axioms of the theory and the calculation—are still waiting to be made explicit. As the term 'calculation' used by Boudon evokes, in my view, a mathematical association which is rather too rigorous for my interpretation, it would be more accurate to describe the operation as rules of transformation, as indeed they are, and to rewrite expression (II) in the following way:

(III) R: $\{A, App\ (S)\} \longrightarrow Str\ (S)$

where R is a mapping of *A* and *App* (*S*) into *Str* (*S*), i.e., R represents the rules of transformation and the operation is one of *decoding*. I can now proceed to elucidate *A*, the axiomatic frame-work, and R, the rules of transformation.

The fundamental axioms of structuralism are:

(*a*) that the human mind has a innate capacity for structuring knowledge (where knowledge is conceived of in the widest possible sense to include everything we are aware of);

(*b*) that all forms of human behaviour are also codes;

(*c*) that the analysis of the totality of relations making a universe of discourse is imperative;

(*d*) that these relations can be reduced to binary oppositions;

(*e*) that the changes within the system are accounted for by laws of transformations; and finally,

(*f*) that the system is self regulating.

These axioms are fundamental to any structural investigation and represent the general theoretical framework within which this study is embedded. However, to supplement these axioms, further premises relevant to my specific area of investigation must be postulated. To this purpose some notions which are derived from Set Theory are used. They are further clarified in the appendix to this chapter.

Let P denote the set of all advertisements, then:

1. P can be partitioned into subsets P_i ($i = 1, 2, \ldots, n$), $P_i \subset P$, which are classified by the products they advertise, such that

$$\bigcap_{i=1}^{n} P_i = P_1 \cap P_2 \cap \ldots \cap P_n = \phi$$

2. In each subset of advertisements P_i, or in any member of this set, it is possible to identify constituent units, α, β, γ, . . . etc.

3. For each constituent unit it is possible to identify, either explicitly or by implication, its binary opposition. (The nature and type of binary oppositions to be considered in the following chapters will be elucidated in the sequel.)

4. There exists a binary operation, symbolically denoted by (:), designating the positional ratio between each constituent unit and its binary opposition.

5. The set of all positional ratios (i.e. pairs of binary oppositions) can be ordered by a relation, symbolically denoted ($\simeq$), by reference to which the positional ratios between α and β can be related to the positional ratio between γ and δ, etc. (In symbols this is expressed as $\alpha : \beta \simeq \gamma : \delta$, etc.)

It will become apparent, as a result of the analysis in the following chapter, that the ordering relation defined in postulate (5) is reflexive, symmetric and transitive and, hence, it is an equivalence relation. Furthermore, I will try to show that under the binary operation defined in postulate (4), the system under consideration possesses a semi-group structure. It should be noted, however, that these two conclusions are brought in and their validity shown for completeness' sake only and will be left at that.

Some points must still be clarified. It follows from axiom (1) that a distinction is drawn between advertisements for different products, but not necessarily between advertisements for different brands. As a rule, the static analysis was done by product groups and the dynamic one by brand or house names. In the first case, all butter, for instance, was regarded as one product and no distinction was made between Anchor or Lurpak. Likewise, baby foods were taken as one group even though the advertisements themselves were from Heinz, Gerber, Farley's, Cow and Gate, and Robinson's.* In the case of TV advertising, I was constrained by the material as well as by the final object, which compelled me to look at sets of advertisements for one brand name at a time, though not necessarily at the same product. The reasons for this will be made clear in Chapter 4.

Three considerations made the adoption of the general partitioning procedure imperative. First, it was previously assumed that in order to analyse a 'story' it is necessary to take into account all known versions (in practice, as many as it is possible to find). If each advertisement for a brand or for a product is regarded as one version, it follows that the more versions one collects the easier it becomes to identify the constituent units and the relations among them.

Second, the number and the breadth of the advertisements available for each brand in the static case (magazine advertising) provided such a fragmentary view of the system, whose shape and nature were as yet unknown, that more specimens were needed of the same general genre to assist in deciphering the message. Many advertisements on their own and in themselves define only little bits of the structure and consequently it becomes absolutely necessary to have more 'stories' told of the same product in order to arrive at the structural resolution of the basic theme. Whether this repetitive story is told by one company or a few competitive firms is, from the point of view of symbolic perception, quite immaterial.

The third consideration revolves around the big question of what constitutes a legitimate system of analysis. A whole chapter is devoted to this problem. I would merely say here that a structure is only decipherable if all the advertisements belonging to the same *product field* are analysed. The minimal system is the system of appearances of a product field; in other words, all the representations of all the brands which make up the product group. On the other hand, all the images of a single competitive brand alone never form a system. So, all the commercials for air

---

* These are all names of British manufacturers.

25

travel, for instance, will form one legitimate system, but all the commercials for Pan Am alone, will never form an admissible system. Consequently, if one wishes to decipher an advertising system, one simply must take into account all the ads of the product group in question. In general and in accordance with the premises of the theory, it is expected that each set of advertisements will exhibit at the very least one of the possible realizations of the underlying structure.

Postulates (2) and (3) state that, having identified the constituent units, the binary opposition of each one of them either 'physically' exists within the considered sub-set of advertisements, or is implied by the existing constituent unit. In the majority of cases every attempt is made to discover the binary opposition in the material itself. Indeed, the compulsion to find such binary segments constitutes a very important check on the completeness of the data, for in most cases it forces one to go back to the material and look again for the 'missing' elements. In this fashion the natural tendency for selectivity is effectively curbed.

The second part of expression (III) which still demands a clarification are the rules of transformations. These are defined as follows:

1. A sub-set P_i of P, $P_i \subset P$, is delineated.
2. For each advertisement, Ad_j, that belongs to P_i, $Ad_j \in P_i$ (where ϵ means 'belongs to'), constituent units are identified. This is done by first listing all the attributes of the advertised product, and secondly by eliminating all the redundant elements, resulting in a non-repetitive set of constituent units where each appears just once.
3. The aggregated set of constituent units is then partitioned in such a way that each constituent unit is associated with its binary opposition, the latter being present either as a result of rule (2) or as a logical derivative.
4. Reduction is performed on the ordered set derived in (3) to establish an homologous ordered set; the latter being the Exhaustive Common Denominator (ECD) of the former.

Thus $Str (S_i)$, the structure of sub-set P_i, can be obtained. By virtue of this procedure expression (III) is the *decoding* expression. A graphic description of the process is given on page 27.

This procedure is rather similar to the one suggested by Lamb in his discussion of stratificational grammar. He uses the term encoding where I would use the term decoding:

> The system presented here is called stratificational because one of its chief features is the recognition of a series of strata or structural layers in language. A language, by its nature relates sounds (or graphs, i.e. marks on paper or the like) to meanings, and this relationship is a very complex one which turns out to be analysable in terms of a series of code-like systems, each of which connects two neighbouring strata. The topmost structural stratum, the sememic, has units directly related to meaning. These sememics may be thought of as encodable into units of the next lower stratum, which in turn are themselves encodable, and so on, until one comes out with units directly related to speech or writing (i.e. with phonemes or graphemes) . . . The code relating each pair of neighbouring strata is a set of *stratificational rules*.[12]

In summary, beginning with certain axioms, I proceeded to develop rules of transformation and by employing them on the apparent characteristics of the system, App (S) (the sample of advertisements), the Exhaustive Common Denominators were derived. These ECD's may be regarded as the structure of the system.

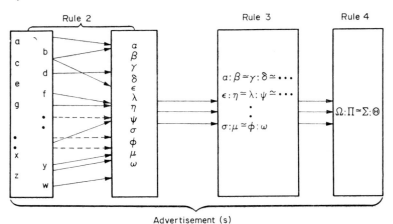

Fig. 1. The transformation process—R: $\{A,\ App(S)\} \to Str(S)$

One problem still demands some elucidation. Clearly, the importance of the binary oppositions cannot be overestimated in the context of this approach. Yet the pairs are almost never as well defined as they are in logic or mathematics. Nevertheless even from this rather strict point of view, the usage of the term in this study is not entirely divorced from the interpretation it is given in the more exact sciences. Also, it might be emphasized again that the material is human perception, which may conceive of two items as being diametrically opposed to each other, even though from the point of view of their dual meaning they cannot 'logically' be ascertained as 'real' oppositions. In spite of the fact that the classifications may be 'wrong' on one level of reasoning, on the level that matters in terms of meaningful human communication they are correct.

There are three types of oppositions: the digital type; the analogue type (graded scale), and the converse type.

1. The first type of opposition is the truly binary and therefore can be modelled on the digital computer. The relations between the digits b_1 and b_2 are such that:*

   (a) $b_1 \cap b_2 = \phi$ (they are mutually exclusive), and
   (b) $b_1 \cup b_2 \subseteq M$ (they are exhaustive).

2. The second type of oppositions, which may be called, following Lyons, antonyms, 'behave' like two opposites. However, their sense of oppositeness is derived from the fact that they express different degrees of intensity on the same comparative scale.[13] The sense in which they are employed is graded, precisely because they both belong to the same implicit dimension and are understood by reference to an implicit norm. This type of opposition is designated by the following conditions: c_1 and c_2 are terms where

   (a) $c_1 \cap c_2 \neq \phi$ (they are not mutually exclusive), and
   (b) $c_1 \cup c_2 \subseteq M$ (they are exhaustive).

* The symbols are customarily defined as: $\cup$ = union or conjunction; $\cap$ = intersection or disjunction; $\subset$ = included; $\subseteq$ = included and equal to; ϕ = the empty set; M = universe of discourse. For further clarification reference should be made to the summary at the end of this chapter.

This second case expresses gradual change or grades of change (more/less) and is in fact modelled on the analogue computer.

An example may clarify both the similarities and the differences between the two cases. The scheme used is an adaptation of a semantic model suggested by Greimas.[14] The two terms 'beautiful' and 'ugly' may be viewed in the following way: there is something which is more beautiful or less beautiful as there is equally something which is more or less ugly. However, something which is not beautiful is not necessarily ugly and vice versa a thing which is not ugly is not necessarily beautiful. It follows that ugly cannot be considered as the binary opposition of beautiful but only as the binary opposition of not ugly, and the same applies of course to beautiful. We may, then, draw the following figure:

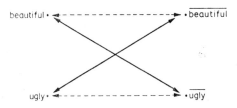

The double arrows denote bi-laterality. In this model, beautiful is contrary to ugly and beautiful is contradictory to $\overline{beautiful}$. Relations of contrariness are graded oppositions while relations of contradiction are digital. The system (beautiful, $\overline{beautiful}$) is, therefore, contrary to the system (ugly, $\overline{ugly}$). The dotted lines designate disjunction of contradictions (mutual exclusivity) and the solid lines disjunction of contrariness (gradation). Thus, returning to cases (1) and (2) above, beautiful and $\overline{beautiful}$ or ugly and $\overline{ugly}$ are b_1 and b_2 respectively, while beautiful and ugly are c_1 and c_2 respectively. The last pair admits cases where something may be neither beautiful nor ugly, or alternatively both beautiful and ugly. Such a model has many diverse applications and I may have occasion to come back to it in due course.

3. In the third case, d_1 and d_2 are two terms where:

(a) $d_1 \cap d_2 = \phi$ (the terms are mutually exclusive), and
(b) $d_1 \cup d_2 \subset M$ (the terms do not exhaust the universe).

Thus, the terms are like (1) in that they are mutually exclusive, and unlike (1) or (2) in that they do not exhaust the universe of discourse. Such terms are for example the pair 'father' and 'mother'. They are mutually exclusive because under no condition could one be transformed into the other, but since the conjunction of the two terms is only included in the universe but is not equal to it, father and mother are neither contradictions nor contraries, but perhaps can be said to be converse to each other.[15] The fact that they do not make up the whole universe means that one could argue with the same conviction that mother, for instance, is the converse of daughter, or daughter-in-law, or grandmother, and so on.

Boudon argues that his formula II (the one used in this analysis) 'expresses the procedure by which the "structure" of the system is obtained',[16] while his formula I (see page 22 above) 'describes the testing procedure by which one ascertains that a theory is really acceptable'.[17] In other words, formula I tests the analysis for validity. The advantage of this test is that it is both direct and convenient in the sense that, when applicable, it may expose a theory as false rather easily. When for various reasons it is impossible to apply this test, it does not mean that the theory is wrong, but only that one has to look necessarily for other means to verify it. In this case it is possible, in principle, to apply this test, since theoretically one may transform back from the Exhaustive Common Denominator to the apparent characteristics of the system.

Naturally, many questions may be raised concerning the reliability and validity of this approach and, by implication, of the results based on it. To this I can only say that the method shares its weaknesses with similar procedures. Whatever virtues it may have are due to the fact that it complies with certain rules of analysis and because it is consistent within itself. It follows principles which were established both in anthropology and linguistics and suggests an approach to the problem at hand.

Boudon has convincingly argued that no one universal structural analysis can exist, but that 'while the structure of a system is always the result of a hypothetico-deductive theory applied to the given system, certain *constraints*—imposed by the specific nature examined—mean that these theories can take extremely diverse forms . . .'[18]; 'the success met within its (structuralist) application depends to a very large extent upon the object analysed'.[19] Whether in the end the analysis seems convincing or not is left to the reader to decide.

Appendix: Summary of some relevant concepts of set theory

1. A *set* is a well defined collection of objects called elements or members of the set. If an object x is a member of a set A, denoted by $x \epsilon A$, x is said to *belong* to A. All elements belonging to a particular set have in common a well-defined property. For example, if being a four-legged animal is the qualifying property for being an element of the set A, then, among others, horse, cow, dog and cat belong to A.

2. If every element of a set B is also a member of a set A, then B is called a sub-set of A, denoted by $B \subset A$. Considering the above example, if $A = \{$horse, cow, dog, cat$\}$ and $B = \{$cow, cat$\}$, then $B \subset A$.

3. Generally all sets are likely to be sub-sets of a so-called *universal set* or *universe of discourse*. For the above example, the universe of discourse is the set whose members are all four-legged animals.

4. A set which contains no elements is called the *empty* or *null* set, denoted by the symbol ϕ. For example, if A is the set of people in the world who are immortal, and since there is no evidence to the contrary, A is an empty set.

5. If A and B have no elements in common, then A and B are said to be *disjoint*. For example, if $A = \{x, y, z\}$ and $B = \{r, s, t\}$, A and B are disjoint.

6. The *union* or *conjunction* of sets A and B is a set C all of whose elements belong to A or to B or to both. The union is denoted by $C = A \cup B$. For example, if $A = \{a, b, c\}$ and $B = \{x, y, z, c\}$ then $C = A \cup B = \{a, b, c, x, y, z\}$. Note in this example that the order in which members are written down is irrelevant.

7. The *intersection* or *disjunction* of sets A and B is a set C all of whose elements are *common* to A *and* B. The intersection is denoted by $C = A \cap B$. For example, let $A = \{1, 2, 3, 4, 5, 6\}$ and $B = \{2, 4, 6, 7\}$, then $C = A \cap B = \{2, 4, 6\}$.

    Remark: It follows from (4) and (7) that, if A and B have no common element, then they are disjoint and their intersection is the empty set: $A \cap B = \phi$.

31

8. *A binary relation*, R, from a set *A* to a set *B* assigns to each pair of elements (*a*, *b*), where *a* ∈ *A* and *b* ∈ *B*, exactly one of the following statements:

    (i) '*a* is related to *b*', denoted *aRb*.

    (ii) '*a* is not related to *b*', denoted *a$\not{R}$b*.

For example, marriage is a relation from the set *M* of men to the set *W* of women since, for any men *m* ∈ *M* and any women *w* ∈ *W*, either *m* is married to *w* or *m* is not married to *w*.

9. A relation R in a set *A* is called *reflexive* if for every element of *A*, *aRa*.

10. A relation R in a set *A* is called *symmetric* if whenever *aRb* implies *bRa*, *a* and *b* being elements of *A*.

11. A relation R in a set *A* is called *transitive* if for every *a*, *b*, and *c* being elements of *A*, *aRb* and *bRc* implies *aRc*.

12. A relation R is called an *equivalence relation* if R is reflexive, symmetric and transitive.

The following example will serve to illustrate (9) to (12). Let *A* be the set of all persons living in a block of flats and let the relation R mean 'has the same surname as'. Clearly, for every *a* ∈ *A*, *aRa* is true, i.e., person *a* has the same surname as person *a* (which is he himself) and, hence, due to (9), R is reflexive. Next, for every person in the block of flats, if *a* has the same surname as *b*, then *b* has the same surname as *a*. Hence, due to (10), R is symmetric. Finally, for every triad of persons *a*, *b* and *c*, if a has the same surname as *b*, and *b* has the same surname as *c*, then *a* has the same surname as *c*, and, due to (11), R is transitive. Hence, due to (12), R is an equivalence relation. Note that if we replace R to read 'is the brother of', then, although this relation is reflexive and transitive, it is not symmetric since if *a* is the brother of *b*, *b* is not necessarily the brother of *a* but can be his sister.

References

1. See, for example: C. Metz, 'Propositions méthodologiques pour l'analyse du film', *Information sur les Sciences Sociales*, vol. 7, No. 4 (August 1968); also Metz, 'La grande syntagmatique du film narratif', *Communications*, no. 11 (1966); Metz, 'Au-delà de l'analogie, l'image', *Communications*, no. 15 (1970); U. Eco, 'Semiologie des messages visuels', ibid.; V. Morin, 'Le dessin humoristique', ibid.; J. Bertin, 'La graphique',

ibid.; L. Marin, 'La description de l'image', ibid.; E. K. Maranda, 'The logic of riddles' in P. Maranda and E. K. Maranda, eds, *Structural Analysis of Oral Tradition* (Philadelphia: University of Pennsylvania Press, 1971).

2. See, for example: L. Festinger, *A Theory of Cognitive Dissonance* (Tavistock Publications, 1959); E. Katz and P. F. Lazarsfeld, *Personal Influence* (Illinois: Free Press of Glencoe, 1955); D. Riesman, N. Glazer, *The Lonely Crowd* (New Haven, Conn: Yale University Press, 1961); E. M. Rogers, *Diffusion of Innovation* (New York: The Free Press, 1962); M. Rokeach, *Beliefs, Attitudes and Values* (San Francisco: Jossey-Bass, 1969); M. McLuhan, *The Mechanical Bride* (Routledge & Kegan Paul, 1967); McLuhan, *The Gutenberg Galaxy* (Routledge & Kegan Paul, 1962); McLuhan, *The Medium is the Message* (Harmondsworth: Allen Lane, 1967), McLuhan, *Cliché and Archetype* (New York: Pocket Books, 1970).

3. M. Weber, *The Protestant Ethic and the Spirit of Capitalism* (Allen & Unwin, 1930); Weber, *The Sociology of Religion* (Methuen, 1965); Weber, G. Roth and C. W. Wittich, eds., *Economy and Society* (New York: Bedminster Press, 1968); P. A. Sorokin, *Social and Cultural Mobility* (Illinois: Free Press of Glencoe, 1959); N. J. Smelser, *Theory of Collective Behaviour* (Routledge & Kegan Paul, 1962); Smelser, *The Sociology of Economic Life* (New Jersey: Prentice-Hall, 1963), Smelser, ed., *Readings on Economic Sociology* (New Jersey: Prentice-Hall, 1965); T. Veblen, *The Theory of the Leisure Class* (Allen & Unwin, 1925).

4. For instance, J. Durand, 'Rhétorique et image publicitaire', *Communications* no. 15 (1970); G. Péninou, 'Physique et métaphysique de l'image publicitaire', ibid.; R. Barthes on the same subject in *Communications*, no. 4 (1964–65).

5. Both references 1 and 4.

6. J. Piaget, *Structuralism*, p. 7.

7. C. Lévi-Strauss, *Structural Anthropology* (Allen Lane, 1968), p. 279.

8. Ibid.; Lévi-Strauss, *The Raw and the Cooked*, Mythologiques I (Paris: Plon, 1964), pp. 98, 199, 307; D. G. MacRae, Introduction to R. Boudon, *The Uses of Structuralism* (Heinemann, 1972), p. ix.

9. C. Lévi-Strauss, *Structural Anthropology*, p. 211.

10. R. Boudon, op. cit., pp. 72–7.

11. Ibid., p. 72.

12. S. M. Lamb, *Outline of Stratificational Grammar* (Washington: Georgetown University Press, 1966), p. 3.

13. J. Lyons, *Introduction to Theoretical Linguistics* (Cambridge University Press, 1968), pp. 463, 465–7.

14. A. J. Greimas and F. Rastier, 'The interaction of semiotic constraints', in Yale French Studies *Game, Play, Literature*, no. 41, 1968, pp. 86–105.

15. J. Lyons, op. cit., pp. 467–9.

16. R. Boudon, op. cit., p. 99.

17. Ibid.

18. Ibid., p. 52.

19. Ibid., p. 63.

3. Immobility and expression: static advertising

Is it like the sculpture lurking in the stone, waiting to be released by interface, by the shock of encounter with some other word or instrument?   McLuhan

In the production-consumption process advertising is commonly thought of as a mediator between the manufacturer and the consumer. It seeks to convert a non-user into a user and to perpetuate usage, once it is achieved, through reinforcement. To accomplish this, advertising has to perfect what Jacques Durand calls '*l'art de la parole feinte*'[1] and it is partly on account of this role, of the loud, mercenary and bewitching go-between, that advertising is frowned upon in certain social circles. There are of course more serious reasons for this. Professor MacRae has suggested that advertising is degraded not only as a human activity but even as a subject for sociological research because it is regarded as a menace to the still very strong cultural tradition of thrift and economy propagated by the Puritan ethic.[2] And last and very significantly, advertising is challenged as a perpetrator and exponent of a certain social and economic order.

To me, however, it is precisely the middle role which is of great interest. Advertising is indeed a mediator, not only simply between the producer and the consumer or the persuader and the persuaded but also, and this may be the crucial point for those who concern themselves with communication and perception systems, between the abstract and the concrete. Like any other mediator it is a bridge between two poles and while embodying both it is exclusively neither. For instance, an androgyny is a mediator par excellence for it is the embodiment of both the feminine and the masculine principles of existence, and while being neither male nor female, it is both. Advertising in a less dramatic fashion is essentially the same for it has a dual role which transforms, in the same medium, the abstract into the concrete and the concrete into the abstract: the traffic is two-way but the road one.

How is this transformation accomplished? First and most fundamental, the process is inherent in the realization of the activity itself: to propagate consumption of things (concrete), advertising acts by putting in motion a range of abstract means, from images and symbols to values, beliefs and attitudes. Though devoted to the advocacy of goods and services, the things propagated are never part of the advertisement, only their abstract representation is, their 'story', their picture or their sign. Accepting that only a mental concept of a product is possible within an advertisement, another important fact presents itself, for of the two available possibilities of representation, the verbal and the visual, one is more abstract (the narrative), the other more concrete (the photograph). Indeed, if a product and its *image publicitaire* were to form one system, then the photographed product could mediate between the concrete and the narrated. Still on this concrete/abstract dimension, the photographed product enjoys a middle position between the product as 'storied' about and any specific realization of it in real life.

This is not all. Products never exist in a void; they are aimed at people, in fact at rather specific groups of people, which are referred to as market segments. However, in the same way that concrete goods are never part of an advertisement, so concrete users may never participate in it and only their surrogate may gain admittance. It is because of this simple minded fact that the degree of versatility and flexibility of the user image is so extensive. The represented product could never be allowed to be distorted too much because eventual recognition in the market place must not be jeopardized. However, the mirror image of the user is a different matter. On the most abstract level one may find emperors and queens, mythological figures and Olympian gods. This level is the most abstract because it is the most detached, completely and absolutely unattainable. Next come all those 'beautiful people', men and women, young and old, that though one can never hope to become *them*, one can nevertheless strive to emulate them. And finally, on the most concrete level, are those descriptions of the consumer which attempt to be as literal and as 'close to life' as possible.

Within the advertising system, and if one is to confine oneself for the moment to the various combinations of the mental representation of products and users only, it is apparent that the most abstract form of realization possible is for either no user *or* no product to appear. Following our previous analysis the circumstance of 'no product' is more abstract than that of 'no user'. Conversely the most concrete possibility is for both product and user to appear. Within those two broad possibilities the more (or less) abstract form is determined in accordance with the observations outlined above. In Figure 2, the degree of

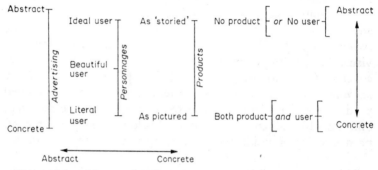

Fig. 2. Advertising as a mediator between the abstract and the concrete

abstractness and concreteness is expressed from left to right, where the movement to the right increasingly becomes more concrete. This is true both with regard to the top axis and the bottom axis. The distance between the abstract and the concrete is manifested in the movement from top to bottom where the vertical differential between the abstract and the concrete gradually decays.

It is thus perhaps fair to say that advertising is shown to be a process of mediation, not just in the commercial sense, but also and most importantly on the perceptual plane. If one conceives of advertising as a mediator between the abstract and the concrete, and if this proposition is correct, then inevitably this fundamental principle of organization will manifest itself in every aspect and on every level at which the advertising game is being played.

Naturally, the possibilities inherent in this structure could be further elaborated. For instance, in advertisements for things (as distinct from services) there is a clear distinction between the 'front' and the 'back', and users are normally part of the background.*[3] Now, if the product is the mental representation conjured up by the advertisement and supported by the story and the picture, then the background, which includes users in their various settings, colour, accessories, layout and so on, is the signifier. In other words, the advertised product is the signified to which the background acts as a signifier; together they form a sign. Thus, following Saussure, to form a signifying unit, both are essential, and as they are a unity there is no sense in asking which is more important or necessary than the other. The background formulation is as important to the front as the two sides of the coin are to each other. It is of the very essence of the system to possess this aspect without which it could not have constituted a signifying totality. If this is correct, then the relations into which the back and the front can enter are extremely important. For instance, the way in which the product (the front) relates to the back is crucial to the evocation of sense, to say nothing of the manner in which it contributes to the arresting power of the advertisement and the perceptual mechanism it employs to capture the eye.

I have maintained before that the formalistic aspects of the advertising system are of little interest to me. The temptation, however, to pursue this a little further is considerable. I shall therefore confine myself to a few comments only by way of illustration.

The spatial relations between the background and the object in static advertising may take the following forms:

(a) Equivalence ($B = P$): the background and the product have an equal status, it is thus impossible to know which one is being advertised unless a reference is made to the text (e.g. normally proportioned cup of coffee and a packet of cigarettes).

---

* Things become rather more complicated when services are advertised as it is possible to present the actual service only indirectly. In this sense the representation of services in advertising is always more abstract than goods advertisements.

(*b*) Background is larger than product (*B>P*): The product proportions may vary.

(*c*) Background is smaller than product (*B<P*).

(*d*) Background only: product is implied through the verbal support and much is left to the imagination. Borrowing from the comics these relations may be visualized in the following manner:

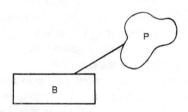

(*e*) Product only, where the type of user is vaguely suggested by abstract references such as lighting, name, colour, etc. This is in a way the converse of the previous case.

Obviously, each one of these could easily be placed in terms of its relative abstractness or concreteness on Figure 2.

Finally, another group of relations between the background and the product may be explored to detect the ways in which they are made compatible with each other and the manner in which they draw upon the spatial relations outlined above.

Background and product can be:

(*a*) Complementary: in this case equivalence relations may be preferred (e.g. cigar and wine).

(*b*) Contradictory (e.g. cigarettes and nature). It is not surprising that in this type of advertisements, while the background envelops the product to convey the idea that the product is part of something better, bigger, and so on, the product itself may be over-sized precisely in order to avoid this complete absorption.

(*c*) Comparative or similar, where by a rule of association the product is deemed to be like other suggestive things and used by an attractive personnage. An extensive list of this type of possibilities was provided by Durand.[4] Most of these relations are metaphorical.

(*d*) Integration: mostly metonymic. Either the reader completes an image by mentally providing the rest of the picture, or the product is represented as an integral part of the background in such a way that the result of using the product and the product itself are confused (e.g. lipstick on face, shampooed hair).

(*e*) Cyclical relations, where the background and object alternate in such a way that they create an endless circle of signification. (For example, in 'Bright and Bold' the girls signify the paint, the paint signifies the walls, the walls signify the girls and so on ad infinitum. Then the leaping movement of the girls signifies the brightness of the colours and in its turn this brightness is emphasized against dark irregular contours of walls.)

The whole argument so far may be summarized in a schema where the more likely interdependences between spatial relations and associative relations are depicted by solid lines.

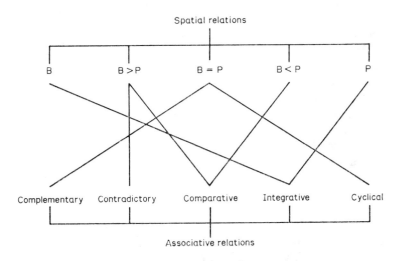

It was maintained before that advertising is conceived of as a mediator par excellence. It is perhaps less apparent that every part of an advertisement is also a mediator in its own right. The background is simultaneously a part of real life and part of the reality of the advertisement; equally, the pictured product is both signified by the advertisement and signifies the real product; thus it, like the background, is also a mediator between concrete and imagined reality.

I may stop here, after a rather long detour, to turn in a different direction and pursue the main goal of my analysis. All judgements and theoretical implications will be reserved till the two demonstrations are completed. I will simply follow here the actual experiment, beginning with the case of static advertising.

One hundred copies of two women's magazines, *Woman* and *Woman's Own*, appearing in 1970/71 are the source of the sample of advertisements. These two journals were selected because they are the two most popular women's magazines in England and consequently are thought to represent well the taste of the public in the widest sense of the word. The actual products chosen were determined by the interest I have in the most ordinary purchasing behaviour, the purchase of routine, ordinary, repetitive, mundane and low-priced products, in other words, in everyday consumption. In the first demonstration the main object of the analysis is to test the hypothesis that it is possible, on the basis of clues existing on the surface level, to deduce the structural resolution of the theme through a process of decoding.

At the very least, then, one must start from the assumption that it is permissible to regard a complex of advertisements for one product category as one system, or indeed as a sub-system in the total universe of advertising. I am not concerned here with surface messages peculiar to specific brands but with the underlying structure of the system as a whole. In the total universe of product tales, each advertisement is regarded as one version. If the whole system is one big jigsaw puzzle then each version provides a fragment which constitutes one part in the ultimate reconstruction of the total picture. The actual reconstruction is not as straightforward as it seems for even when a large number of versions is put at one's disposal, the degree of 'noise' in the system is such that any deciphering proves a trying exploit. To surmount the interference with the message a very high degree of repetition or redundancy is necessary. The persistence of the big hammer of recurrence is essential in order that the message on both levels will be able to push its way through the perceptual barriers.

A final remark, before turning to the actual exposition, concerns the order of presentation. As the system is one closed universe of discourse, the door on which one chooses to knock first is immaterial. Whatever road one takes first, at the end of the journey all the pieces must fall into place; and a full circle must be accomplished when the correct arrangement is found. I will have further occasions to return to this basic issue concerning the total universe of all advertising later. At this stage, however, the demonstration will be confined to a limited number of products, whose defining principles are based on oppositions which, in this specific case, find their natural expression in the game of contrasts between a product and its competitors.

Peace : war ≃ butter : margarine

Lévi-Strauss has suggested a typology, consisting of a limited number of dimensions, on the basis of which every food product may be classified.[5] A detailed summary of these dimensions are provided below (page 47). The dimensions describe every conceivable form of all known foods and involve such scales as marked/not marked (i.e. hot, salty, bitter or mild, milky, etc.); central/peripheral (i.e. main dish versus first course; meat versus vegetables, etc.); maximal/minimal transformation (i.e. degree of proximity to natural condition) as well as others. In the case under consideration two facts are immediately apparent: butter differs from all possible competitors on one dimension only, the dimension of the maximal/minimal transformation; namely, butter is somehow perceived to be a natural product. And secondly, of all possible competing products, the most important one is margarine.

If there is only a limited amount of truth in the observation that butter differs from margarine only in the degree of transformation or distance between some criterion of origin and the final product, then the fact that butter as a rule is equated with nature, *basic* goodness, soil and land, green pastures, countryside, cows and milk; and margarine with change, the advancement of science and vegetable oils is hardly surprising (e.g. Buttercook, Anchor, Flora). Indeed, the only way to emphasize the naturalness of butter against the artificiality of margarine is to design an image which is as close as possible to the origins.

Margarine advertisements start from a different premise. Being perceived to be further removed from nature than butter, they are inevitably compelled to emphasize the modern scientific aspects of the product and to provoke an image of health and well-being which exists in spite of the product's remoteness from the source. This basic dilemma is expressed on all levels: background, users, form and verbal approach. The fact that such a prediction could be made on the basis of the theoretical and universal food typology proposed by Lévi-Strauss is interesting in itself, for the inevitable conclusion is that contrary to normal expectation and before any advertising took place the number of possible ideas had already been restricted in ways which are by no means apparent at first sight.

The argument so far has been that the position of two competing food products on the dimensional typology is bound to express itself in the differential manner in which they are treated in the advertisements. But advertising does more than that. One particular set of advertisements for butter is worth recording in some detail as it provides a clear opportunity for demonstrating the structuralist method at work. In this set margarine is explicitly mentioned as a competing product for which people pay a few pennies less. The advertisements depict simple situations in which the use of butter is recommended. For instance, a child having breakfast just before going to school; a father reading the paper, eating a slice of bread and butter watched by his child; a barbecue party of young people; a couple of old people, she is knitting and he is having a bun. The message is made up of theme and copy and explores the relations in which butter is said to be:

> concord for the young
> content for the old
> care for father
> love for children

It will be noticed that the left-hand side of the formulae include several variations on the same underlying theme. Very little information will be added to these words by including further elements of the same type such as affection, satisfaction, happiness and so on. In this sense, the information conveyed by the left-hand side is already sufficient for the realization of the underlying theme and any addition is redundant. This type of redundancy is very usual in any communication system.

On the right-hand side, the last word of each phrase, one crucial element is missing. The advertisements explore four possibilities, namely, youth, old people, father and children. The only possibility which is not explicitly portrayed is that of mother. It is reasonable to assume that this omission is deliberate rather than accidental, and is due to the advertiser's subtle intention to let every housewife participate in the campaign in the role of the missing woman. All the elements on the left are of integrative nature, and all the elements on the right together with the missing representation of mother, now amount to the whole population (young + old + father + mother + children). The fundamental message may be summarized as asserting that butter symbolizes peace, integration and cohesiveness for the people who use it.

However, this is only the first part of the motion, as butter has also a competitor to fight—margarine. If this is taken into account the complete argument reads as follows:

$$
\begin{array}{llll}
\text{butter : margarine} & \simeq \text{dear} & : \text{cheap} & \simeq \\
& \simeq \text{concord} & : \text{protest} & \simeq \\
& \simeq \text{content} & : \text{discontent} & \simeq \\
& \simeq \text{care} & : \text{negligence} & \simeq \\
& \simeq \text{love} & : \text{hate} &
\end{array}
$$

where : means 'is to' and $\simeq$ means 'like'.

It is here that the previous comments concerning repetition become clear. It will be remembered that in accordance with the transformation rules elucidated in Chapter 2, all redundancy is excluded before the elements of the pure non-redundant set are associated in binary relations. At the same time a repetition of a non-synonymous genre manifests itself; a repetition which is in fact a set of variations on the same fundamental theme, and which is designed, as Lévi-Strauss emphasizes elsewhere, to render the basic structure apparent.[6]

Thus, all the elements on the left-hand side of the above expressions belong to the same type, and similarly all the elements on the right-hand side also belong to one type. It is by virtue of this fact that it is possible to perform a reduction on the whole expression and to obtain an exhaustive homologous formula whose elements also enter into binary relations. In accordance with the terminology introduced in the last chapter, the Exhaustive Common Denominator (ECD) is:

$$\text{peace : war} \simeq \text{butter : margarine}$$

This is the final underlying resolution of this set of butter advertisements against margarine. Peace is in the nature of this analogy the signifier of butter, and war is, at least in butter advertisements, the signifier of margarine. Thus, following semiological theory, peace and butter constitute together a sign.[7] Naturally this observation is valid for any analogy which is based on a structure composed of binary relations.

Old : new ≃ baking : spreading

While the underlying resolution of butter advertisements draw the above analogy, what do margarine advertisements do? To use margarine, in the typical case, one must either spread or bake. By accepted culinary tradition margarine enters into a competition with butter mostly as far as spreading is concerned. Baking is typically performed by using margarine rather than butter. It follows that in so far as a reaction is called for in margarine advertisements to butter claims it should be sought for in that part of the campaign which is devoted to spreading.

As expected this is indeed the area in which the battle is being fought but it is conducted in a strange manner. While butter advertisements emphasize uniqueness and exclusivity, margarine advertisements put the accent on closeness, similarity and association with butter, thereby creating an awkward incongruent situation, where:

$$\text{butter} \neq \text{margarine in butter advertisements, and}$$
$$\text{margarine} = \text{butter in margarine advertisements.}$$

In terms of marketing policy this logical inconsistency is simple to understand as the status of butter and margarine is not equal in the market place. Butter advertisements aim at a full control of the market, while margarine is mainly concerned with enlarging its share of the market. However, from the point of view of consumer perception it creates the bizarre situation where margarine advertisements have an effect of a campaign for butter. In so far as butter and margarine are perceived to be 'binary' oppositions, this is neither recognized nor acknowledged, at least by one side.

It was maintained before that within the margarine sub-system the main distinction is drawn between spreading and baking. The analysis on an exceptionally wide range of advertisements for different companies and for different brands (Cookeen, Flora, Stork, Kraft, Echo, Summer County) tend to yield similar results. The non-redundant set of baking is repeatedly associated with reliability, familiarity and success, while spreading is associated with science, novelty, originality and good health.

The surface elements and the members of the non-redundant set are related but are not the same. While it is possible to transform back from the pure set to the realization of the surface as it is possible to travel in the opposite direction, the pure set is already an exhaustive expression of the surface. Even before any decoding has taken place the clues are already there, for nothing can be postulated to exist if it leaves no trace. The keys are always there waiting to be used but because each advertisement, as indeed any other image, already possesses at least one cognitive meaning, this conscious understanding bars the road to the realization of yet another level which exists behind the apparent one and possesses a truth which is no less real. While the constituent units in their correct relations are always there in the advertisements, the true arrangement which expresses their unconscious structure is up to the interested observer to discover.

It will be noticed that of the constituent units mentioned above, novelty versus familiarity and originality versus reliability are perceived to be natural binary oppositions. Success, which is another elementary segment, is specifically defined as a condition resulting from the use of a certain brand of margarine for baking. The success concerns baking and as such it is opposed to a different type of success which results from and is based upon scientific exploration. Furthermore, spreading margarine is associated with health because, says the advertisement, the margarine is made of polyunsaturated fat. In other words, better health depends upon moderation in the consumption of fat as well as the type of fat consumed. At the same time cakes are strongly associated with excess of both fat and carbohydrate and thus could be dangerous to one's health. Pulling together these observations and arranging them in binary equations the following expressions emerge:

$$\text{baking : spreading} \simeq \text{reliability : originality} \qquad \simeq$$
$$\simeq \text{familiarity : novelty} \qquad \simeq$$

$$\simeq \text{success in baking : scientific advance} \simeq$$
$$\simeq \text{excess of fat : moderation of fat}$$

Thus all the attributes related to baking are in essence traditional, including the one which is involuntarily implied (excess), and all the attributes which are related to spreading are a reflection of a modern attitude of mind. Reliability and familiarity are straight-forward traditional social and personal values. Baking success is a particularly festive consumption symbol of the good mother and wife. Similarly, till quite recently, due to the scarcity of expensive protein, starch and fat were considered to be an adequate diet.

The modern concepts express themselves in perfect contrast to the former ones. Originality and novelty are modern social and personal values par excellence. The activities pursued in the kitchen and in the scientific laboratory are conceptually the same: in both, various ingredients are mixed in fixed measures, and are subjected to various processing procedures in order to achieve desired results. In both these results are achieved in various degrees of success and failure. But they have a different object in mind: in the kitchen yet another pastry, a familiar thing, is created and in the laboratory, though ingredients are still being put together, this time it is in order to invent a new thing. The success attached to baking stems from an appreciation of a new reproduction of an old pastry idea while the sense of success in the laboratory is derived from the creation of something new. Finally, moderation is a modern concept of diet while excess is a traditional one. Gaining weight used to be a sign of health and well being. Obesity, unlike today, was not a term of abuse. Nowadays, modern concepts of nutrition advocate balance and restraint. The advertisements thus explore the theme of the new versus the old on at least three different levels in a way which seems to me to identify the Exhaustive Common Denominator (ECD) as:

$$\text{old : new} \simeq \text{baking : spreading}$$

The different levels of reality which are explored by the advertisements cover a wide range of human experience and include personal and social values, a slice of constructive action and concepts of diet and health. The unerring consistency in which the modern version of each of these levels is juxtaposed against the old-fashioned one indicates that one cannot hope to explain away this phenomenon by simply attributing it to the random work of chance. On the contrary, for in spite of the multiplicity of aspects employed the temptation to spread in several directions is resisted and the flow of images persists in its single track. Even chance has its logical boundaries beyond which another explanation must be sought. Let me turn now to regard a somewhat different type of campaign.

Life : death ≃ baby foods : not baby foods

It is not surprising that baby foods, which offer an extremely wide range of foodstuffs many of which reproduce the flavour of popular English dishes, will easily fall into place on the food dimensions suggested by Lévi-Strauss.[8] The dimensions constitute a typology in terms of which any food, raw or processed, could be classified. It would be observed that the maximal/minimal transformation includes in fact the elaborated/not elaborated and the marked/not marked dimensions, which are presented for the sake of completeness. This first abstraction has been greatly improved upon and elaborated in later works, especially in the first and second versions of the culinary triangle, the latter forming the fundamental resolution of structure in *Mythologiques*.[9]

If the first element is marked by + and the second element by x the following summary is obtained for baby foods:

Dimension	Baby foods	Explanation
Internal/external	x	Within or without the mother
Central/peripheral	+x	Main dish, main item of food or not (e.g. main course vs. first course, meat vs. vegetables)
Marked/not marked	x	Hot, salty, etc., or mild, milky, etc.
Elaborated/not elaborated	+	Processed or not
Maximal/minimal transformation	+	Degree of proximity to the natural condition—the case here is a question of texture and form rather than substance and flavour
Hot/cold (food)	+x	
Milky/alcoholic (drink)	+	
Fresh/fermented (fruit)	x	

Naturally, the number of different ways of realizing these dimensions in concrete products is enormous. For baby foods, for instance, breast-feeding introduces a natural point of departure because it represents a null transformation, thus allowing every industrially manufactured food to be easily placed on the minimal/maximal transformation range. Indeed, the progression of foods on this scale tends to correspond to the age of the child, thus creating an homologous trend between the type of food suggested and the physical development of the baby. One Farley's advertisement explores this transformation in an explicit manner. Against a background of a bare breast and a nurtured baby the theme reads: 'the only food he needs before Farley.'

The degree of transformation may be further juxtaposed against other dimensions such as central/peripheral and so on, thus yielding a system of classification with regard to any conceivable foodstuff. The advertisements analysed offer many examples of this type of permutation but detailed exposition does not seem worth while; they all fit into the catalogue of structural oppositions listed above. If this point is accepted there is not much that one may gain by further illustrating it on a long list of products.

It may be interesting, though, to look at another aspect of these advertisements.* The surface explores the themes of happiness, growth, relates facts about baby life, and the versatile nature of the advertised product. It also examines the ways in which the product satisfies some basic demands. The elements of expertise, knowledge, reassurance and confidence are constantly reiterated. They are essential to the establishment of trust with the mother regarding a subject which is extremely sensitive and important to her. Frequent allusions are made to the baby's need for variety, his need for a balanced diet and the way these two factors correspond to condition his healthy growth. Moreover, diet appears to be essential to his general well-being and to have a lasting effect on the relationships between mother and child. These claims are presented as a function of each other in the following manner:

$$\text{balance} = f\ (\text{variety})$$
$$\text{growth} = f\ (\text{variety, balance})$$

* The advertisements analysed are from Gerber, Heinz, Robinson's, Cow & Gate and Farley's.

happy baby = f (variety, happy mother)
happy mother = f (confidence in the range)
variety = range offered

One feature of these statements is of immediate interest. Once the necessary algebraic substitutions are made, starting from the last equality, all the different items are reduced to the offered range of baby foods. It is important to remember that the statements upon which this reduction is based are the product of the collective endeavour of all the advertisers of baby foods, and not the work of a single campaigner. Second, the reduction is performed on the structural level and not on the surface level. In being able to accomplish this the rule set out by Lévi-Strauss concerning the function of repetition is illustrated in a way which is truly gratifying. It is a truism to claim that the purpose of everything in an advertising image is designed to sell the thing advertised. However the crucial fact is that this is accomplished collectively not only on the surface level but also on the level beneath. The individual advertiser, each in the isolation of his own creative imagination, is engaged in a process of profound, collective and unknown interaction.

This is not all. Returning to the constituent units, an idea which is already implied in the series of functions above demands to be expressed. This is:

baby foods : not baby foods $\simeq$ happiness : unhappiness $\simeq$
$\simeq$ growth : decay $\simeq$
$\simeq$ variety : uniformity $\simeq$
$\simeq$ balance : imbalance

If one now proceeds to reduce the two sides of the formulae into the Exhaustive Common Denominator, the fundamental message seems to be:

life : death $\simeq$ baby foods : not baby foods

The left-hand side evokes a picture of life and the right-hand side an image of death. It must be recalled that not so very long ago the incidence of infant mortality was very high. This dreadful fear of death is still shared by all, though it is not discussed much. Advertisers even if they thought about it could never utilize it because of moral and psychological considerations. And yet

49

unbeknowingly to themselves they somehow together, all of them collectively 'put' into the advertisements this most vitally important promise, indeed, the only promise worth making. Simultaneously, the mother receives the message on a level of which she has no conscious cognition, and is reassured.

Moreover, the products themselves are rarely pictured and when they are depicted they are allocated an inconspicuous place. Instead the advertised product is persistently confused with the baby and the stages in his development. The baby becomes the product, 'the beautiful results'; so much so that one advertisement goes so far as to depict a toddler's picture on a can with a real toddler standing on tip-toe to reach the top of the tin. The child inside and the child outside are one and the same. The continuity of life is expressed also by other means. For instance, the analogy is drawn that—grandmother : baby's mother $\simeq$ baby's mother : baby—the cycle of the generations goes on forever. So, while confidence in the range is established on the surface level by reference to nutritious value, hygiene, balance, and so on, the structural level conveys a message of the greatest possible value, that of life itself.

The endogenous : the exogenous $\simeq$ English cheese : not English cheese

In the previous sections the main object of the analysis was to find out whether a group of advertisements for substitutable products could be regarded as one system and therefore reduced to some fundamental themes. I venture now into a more restricted area which explores the possibility of carrying out such an analysis on a campaign for a generic product. Having decided this, my operations are of necessity delimited to the advocacy of one voice and not as before to the advocacy of all advertised brands in one product area. Attention is devoted to two separate campaigns for cheese, and in the first instance the case of the 'Nine Great English Cheeses'.

The non-redundant set runs as follows:

real English cheese = above others
real English cheese = our great British heritage
real English cheese = all the richness of the national character
real English cheese = the green and pleasant land we live in.

The country, the people and the land are the first and most important identification image. There is, however, a second more specific process of integration at work which relates the different kinds of cheese to their county of origin. For instance, English cheese is looming large over the Cliffs of Dover. The cliffs are silver blue, the cheese orange gold. The cheese, like a gate-keeper, watches over the cliffs, the entrance to the country. In another advertisement the cheese is depicted parallel to the mining pits of Wales, and in yet another the cheese towers over an old English town where its peak is equalled only by the church spire: they are the guards of both authenticity and tradition.

It might be observed that, in the absence of an explicitly stated competitor, the binary inferences, though inherent in the above statements, are not openly defined. While, as a rule, elements can always be associated in binary relations, where the proper opposite is then identified by implication, I wish to avoid conjecture as far as possible. To pursue such a procedure is by no means an error, as one half of a unity has no meaning without the other half. However, it is felt that a stronger case could be established if a competing set of advertisements were found in which a response is formulated to the English cheese campaign. Such a directly competing campaign was indeed identified. It is the set of advertisements for New Zealand cheese. It will be observed that the two campaigns are conducted on the same level of generality. That is they both stick to semi generic types, namely, English and New Zealand cheeses without advertising specific brands which originate from these countries. It is this fact which makes the structural analysis possible.

New Zealand Cheddar is presented as a huge cheese oven in which a cheese meal is being cooked. That is, there is a food within a food; the cooking cheese meal is being incubated as it were within the cheese oven. Now, there is no image which is more evocative of the idea of a closed harmonious whole, and there is no unity which is greater or stronger than an image of pregnancy.

If it is considered that the English cheese advertisements attempt to establish the priority of the 'insider' over and against the 'outsider' by identifying cheese with the closed unity of country and land, then a competing product may try to surmount this identity only by evoking an image of unity which is even stronger.

To a certain limited extent the Nine Great English Cheeses pro-voke an image of a generalized mother, Mother Earth, but the real emphasis is focused on national, one may even say patriotic, identification. The game of oppositions is played in a slightly different manner from that in the previous cases. The 'answers' are formulated not against the claims of the nine but against the things they leave unstated, thus:

English cheese	: New Zealand cheese	$\simeq$
$\simeq$ the real thing	: the false thing	$\simeq$
$\simeq$ near	: far	$\simeq$
$\simeq$ fresh	: (stale) fresh in spite of distance	$\simeq$
$\simeq$ conformity	: never varies	$\simeq$
$\simeq$ good by tradition	: $\simeq$ good value for money	

and the ECD is:

the endogenous : the exogenous $\simeq$
English cheese : not English cheese

Perhaps the most interesting feature of the binary relations depicted above is the pair, 'conformity' against 'never varies'. At first sight these seem to be synonymous, and not oppositions. However, in the pure non-redundant set these were the only two elements left. A search for the 'missing' binary opposition proved in vain, and in the absence of new elementary segments which might have helped to solve the situation, I was forced to reconsider the true relations between these units. It was only then that the realization occurred to me that conformity really means 'changing all the time', following the current vogues, and as such to conform does not mean remaining unchanged but indeed the opposite of never varies. This was by no means clear beforehand and the fact that it was literally forced upon me by the structuralist approach has strengthened my faith in it.

The endogenous versus the exogenous is the theme which distinguishes between we and they, the in and the out, *des nôtres* against *des leurs*. It is, perhaps, the most important social demarca-tion—equal in importance only to the one between ego and alter. That it should underlie these advertisements is not very surprising for the whole campaign is not concerned with the inherent characteristics of cheese but with fostering a loyalty to the place in which they are manufactured. It is a campaign designed not only to propagate but also to shield, and to shield not one brand against the other, but the national, the endogenous, against the foreign, the exogenous.

Body + soul = cheese

Let me turn, now, to another single brand campaign for cheese. This case differs from all the previous ones because it is considered in total isolation. The advertisements depict a mother and son in many different domestic situations where cheese always has an important role to play. The mother and boy are invariant, though the costumes, the type of situation, and the usage to which cheese is put change from one advertisement to another.

The advertisements considered as a whole, resemble a cross-word puzzle where the final true answers are unknown till all the squares are filled in correctly. The elements present themselves in different combinations which need to be entangled and untangled and the unerring answer depends very much on the accurate reading of the question. The advertising claim seems to be on the horns of a dilemma: cheese could either be compared with other protein products such as meat, eggs, etc. or the emphasis could be put on the pure and inherent benefits of cheese itself. In these first steps towards a precise definition of the theme the oppositions are formed as follows:

$$\text{cheese} \neq \text{meat}$$
$$\text{and cheese} > \text{meat (where} > \text{means 'is better than')}$$

The reasons given for these claims are a mixture of fact and fantasy:

cheese : meat $\simeq$ easy to prepare : difficult to prepare $\qquad \simeq$
$\qquad\qquad \simeq$ not elaborated : elaborated (e.g.
$\qquad\qquad\qquad\qquad\qquad$ boeuf à la mode en gelée) $\simeq$
$\qquad\qquad \simeq$ good value $\quad$: poor value $\qquad\qquad\qquad \simeq$
$\qquad\qquad \simeq$ happy (boy) $\quad$: unhappy (boy)

While it is possible to relate the last two oppositions through the way the claim is presented (i.e., the boy is happy because he gets his full allocation of pocket money which in turn is made possible by the fact that cheese is less expensive than meat), it is impossible to reduce the whole series of oppositions to an Exhaustive Common Denominator.

Two considerations are in order here. In the first place these oppositions do not represent the whole system but only one limited part of it. Second, precisely because it is impossible to achieve a good definition of the structure by this type of comparison, that the advertisements resort to other possibilities arriving in the end at a new definition which satisfies the conditions set out above in Chapter 2. The question of the goodness of definition as well as the differences between competitive campaigns and single campaigns will be discussed in Chapter 6.

Having failed to achieve a good structural definition by utilizing a single comparative approach, the evocation of images changes direction in the following manner:

cheese for man   = protein (like meat)
cheese for mother   = ideas for meals
cheese for boy   = visions of meals; protein, calcium, bone (would be a muscle man like father)
cheese for woman   = good shape (no starch)

The 'woman' can be any feminine image: a grown up woman, a girl, a mother, a daughter or a sister.

Having surveyed the familial possibilities the advertisements proceed to claim two things:

cheese is food for thought
and, cheese is a body builder

This second claim is detailed as follows:

cheese builds up brain power, ambition, height, muscle and bone

It is suggested that at this stage the fundamental theme becomes apparent. Rather than formulating cheese in contrast to another product in the usual way illustrated above, cheese is here presented as a symbolic union of body and soul. In other words, it becomes a mediator, a unifying force between two polarities. In the statements above everything is a variation or, if one prefers, a series of homologous manifestations of this basic idea. And all the interactions in which cheese takes part are of a mediatory nature.

For men, cheese is perceived as a physical entity while for mother it takes on a spiritual representation. The boy wants cheese in order to become like father, an identification of the flesh. Similarly the woman as a feminine symbol is perceived to be concerned only with her appearance. There is a fusion of souls between mother and son, when they both think cheese, and a union of flesh between father and son where father is the reference image for the boy. Cheese, in its double aspect, is instrumental in both. This is not all. Cheese is said to be a food for thought, a statement which amounts to a true literary ambiguity. It is a food for thought because it is chemically integrated into the brain as it helps in building up its cells.* It is also quite literally a problem to think over, for it not only evokes nice memories but also presents a large number of possible meal ideas to which a decision process must be applied. To crown it all, cheese is a food product which comes from the animal and yet is not the animal (meat) but is like the animal (both protein). As such it is a mediator between milk and meat, between animal and man and, in terms of these advertisements, between body and soul. It is only as such that it could remain unidentified with neither body nor soul and yet embody the idea of both.

This chapter surveyed five static advertising campaigns. It is the first attempt in this work to test the hypothesis that advertising is a communication system to which the structural laws of decoding could be successfully applied. This seems possible, at least as far as magazine advertising is concerned, and I shall now proceed to examine the situation in a different sphere—where a substantial proportion of advertising takes place—that of dynamic advertising.

References

1. J. Durand, 'Rhétorique et image publicitaire', *Communications*, no. 15 (1970), p. 70.

* This claim is not an interpretation, it appears in the actual advertisements.

2. D. G. MacRae, *Ideology and Society* (Heinemann, 1961), pp. 78–9; MacRae, 'Advertising and social structure', *Advertising Quarterly*, vol. I, No. 1 (August, 1964); MacRae, 'The elite and the conspiracy', *Encounter* (March, 1972), pp. 75–80.

3. The concepts of 'front' and 'back' are borrowed from E. Goffman, *The Presentation of Self in Everyday Life* (Allen Lane, the Penguin Press, 1969), Ch. 1, p. 107; see also Goffman, *Behaviour in Public Places* (New York: The Free Press, 1963).

4. J. Durand, op. cit., pp. 70–95.

5. C. Lévi-Strauss, *Structural Anthropology* (Allen Lane, 1968), pp. 86–7. (The list is given on page 47 of this chapter.)

6. Ibid., p. 213; also the Overture to *The Raw and the Cooked*, *Mythologiques* I (Paris: Plon, 1964).

7. R. Jacobson and M. Halle, *Fundamentals of Language* (The Hague: Mouton & Co.), pp. 55–82; F. de Saussure, *Course in General Linguistics* (McGraw-Hill, 1966), pp. 66–70, 111–19; R. Barthes, *Elements of Semiology* (Jonathan Cape, 1967), pp. 35–57; E. K. Maranda, 'The logic of riddles' in P. Maranda and E. K. Maranda, eds, *Structural Analysis of Oral Tradition* (Philadelphia: University of Pennsylvania Press, 1971), pp. 193–4.

8. See reference 5.

9. See C. Lévi-Strauss, 'Le triangle culinaire', *L'Arc*, no. 26, pp. 19–29; Lévi-Strauss, *Mythologiques* II, *Du Miel aux Cendres* (Paris: Plon, 1966), pp. 21–32; and finally in Lévi-Strauss, *Mythologiques* III, *L'Origine des Manières de Table* (Paris: Plon, 1968), 'petit traité d'ethnologie culinaire', pp. 390–411.

4. Mobility and expression: dynamic advertising

So that gesture, not music, not odours, would be a universal language, the gift of tongues rendering visible not the lay sense but the first entelechy, the structural rhythm.   James Joyce

The difference between static and dynamic advertising is in the medium. The intention, the advertised product, the targeting, indeed all aspects of the advertising process, remain unchanged except the mode of expression. Is it possible, one may ask, to proceed from this obvious point to argue with McLuhan that if the medium is the message then the meaning of advertising as a system of perception must vary in some subtle ways when the medium of expression changes?

While there is no doubt that the medium exercises a profound influence on the form the message may take, it is by no means indisputable that it influences the final recognition of the message to the same extent. Indeed, McLuhan himself does not argue this as forcibly as one is led to believe. His insights concerning the issue seem to be misapprehended for two reasons.[1] In the first place many of his critics confuse his contentions regarding form with a pronouncement, indeed, a verdict passed on contents. This is not the case. Advertising material and Picasso's painting (an example which has never failed to irritate McLuhan's opponents) could indeed resort to the same technique, but this fact alone does not make it an artistic creation of the same magnitude, though it undoubtedly establishes a point of reference which, to those who believe that form is all that matters, is most important.

Second, and this is perhaps the crucial point, McLuhan's 'probes' concern the impact the medium in itself has over and above any specific representation on the small screen. It is this 'transcendental' effect which according to McLuhan orders our consciousness in a manner which no individual transmission could possibly accomplish. The influence of television is comparable only to that of the Gutenberg legacy in which, while every written material can be told apart, the collective effect reaches far beyond these idiosyncratic representations to create rational typographic man. It is not that in McLuhan's world individual contents do not exist—they are simply irrelevant.[2]

It is conceded, then, that magazines and television are two distinct media exercising a profound influence on the form the message may take and also that the manner in which the message is transmitted affects the way in which it is perceived. Whether it is possible to deduce from these observations that the final understanding of the message is also affected in ways of which one is unaware, is rather less certain. For instance, is one's apprehension of an image materially modified when the image is registered through the eye alone (magazines), through the ear alone (radio), or through a combination of eye and ear (television); or is it that the auditory is automatically completed by a mental representation of the visual and vice versa? In other words, if the focus of the inquiry remains stubbornly entrenched in the ultimate resolution of theme, is it correct to argue that this final apprehension itself is different, or is it only that the interpretative mechanism of the mind, which is called forth in order to decipher the code, varies when confronted with signals of a different kind? It is likely that media which address themselves to different senses trigger off diverse suitable reactions in the mind which are best equipped to decode them. The process through which the terminal understanding is achieved must not be confused with the final message. They are indifferent to each other.

If these observations are correct they have a special significance for underlying structures. While surface manifestations may evoke conscious models which direct one's attention away from the true course of understanding; innate structures, though necessarily sensitive to the cues presented to them, cannot but respond in a predetermined and regularized manner. It is this interest in the underyling structure, which clamours to break the barriers of consciousness, that makes the search rather involved.

It has been shown before that the invisible dimension could be explored through the correct ordering of the relations among the elements which form a self-sustaining, complete closed system. However, in the course of this pursuit, having devoted my full attention to the syntagmatic chains and to the paradigmatic relations into which their elements enter, the subtle influence of the medium itself was taken for granted. Naturally, the influence of the medium cannot fail to manifest itself because it is interwoven into the very fabric of expression, but specific consideration of the medium itself has so far been neglected. This question is briefly considered now.

At the outset, it is clear that television advertising is much more turbulent than static advertising for one obvious reason: television images are complex representations which simultaneously draw upon several sign systems—the verbal, the visual, the auditory and the locomotive. The regularized points at which these independent systems are allowed to intersect each other, and the constraints imposed on the manner in which their elements are juxtaposed and superimposed one upon the other, are still very largely unknown.

Although large strides have been made in the structural research of verbal systems and to a certain extent in that of visual systems too, very little is known of the structures of complex systems and the ways the separate sub-systems they are made of may intermingle and interact beyond and across the frontiers of their separate existences.[3] The additive approach itself is by no means an uncontroversial issue. A number of prominent semiologists feel very strongly that complex systems cannot be explained by a simple additive process, in which the implicit assumption is that once the rules of every system are separately constructed, the totality of the complex system could be explained as a whole composed of various component parts. On the contrary, according to Metz or Eco for instance, a complex system could well have a distinct set of rules, a unique structure all its own, which is embedded in it and which typifies it and no other. So, in the same way that the second articulation of language is, according to Martinet, the most important feature of natural languages, the third articulation is proposed as the most significant aspect of complex systems.[4]

Before proceeding to the actual analysis it is still necessary to delineate the major differences between static advertising and television commercials which are inherent in the mode of expression itself. These distinguishing features are important for the sole reason that they represent the only difference between the two systems. In so far as the medium in itself exerts any influence on the final perception, the reasons for it are necessarily embedded in these features. A special emphasis is given to the interaction between the medium and human perception.

The medium exercises a determining control over the utilization of codes, the form the image takes and the means through which it is transmitted. It does not, however, control the message itself, which is accidental to the form, the pertinent aspect of the medium. Thus, while the medium determines the form and while the substance is, as it were, external to it, the final message is determined by the interaction between the medium, the content and the recipient.

It is not odd that in the case of magazine advertisements, concentration on theme and copy was sufficient to establish the structure, for it is in the nature of a typographic medium to convey much through a simply organized tool. Also the theme and the copy tend to reinforce each other because they illustrate and reiterate each other; when the theme talks of a shampoo, the copy illustrates it on beautiful hair and when the copy portrays green meadows with peacefully grazing cows, the same theme is evoked in the story.

In dynamic advertising, the interaction between theme and copy is much more complex and therefore equal attention must be paid to the spoken as well as to what may be negatively described as the non-spoken parts of the scene. Because of the greater complexity of dynamic advertisements and the larger amount of information they convey, as well as the more complicated and elaborated ways in which the different parts interact with each other, the deciphering process is more involved. But the role of the student remains unchanged, i.e., to record faithfully every aspect of the advertisements, minute and inconsequential as each may seem, and to put the constituent units in their correct paradigmatic relations.

It is also maintained that the change of medium could not possibly change the underlying structure in the same way that the rules of language can hardly be expected to change when one talks on television or writes a letter. What does change is

Static and dynamic advertising—points of difference

STATIC ADVERTISING	DYNAMIC ADVERTISING
I The image is frozen in a moment of time. Change is ruled out. It is always retrievable. It is there.	I Movement and change are inherent in the medium. The scene is in constant flux. It is a one-off experience: each sequence as well as the whole scene, once projected, is lost. The commercial is irretrievable at will.
II Typographic: mostly lineally ordered syntagms embedded in the Gutenberg legacy. The non-lineal aspects, if any, tend to be confined to the photograph. Addresses itself to the eye only: picture and narrative, by the use of visual and written codes.	II Electronic legacy: addresses itself to the eye and ear. Employs a complex code made up of visual, verbal, written, auditory and locomotive signs. Has a rounded, total appeal to the senses.
III Space manipulation: the spatial relations are essential for producing the referential sense of the image.	III Time and space manipulation, the temporal dimension like movement, is peculiar to television. These two aspects often overlap and, together with sound, they are the defining characteristics of the medium.
IV Man supremacy: (a) The reader determines the pace and order of communication. The audience is free.	IV Man-machine relationships: (a) The machine determines the pace and order of the communication. The audience is captive, being caught in a pause between two attractive sequences.
(b) The setting is less determining and less conditioning because the reader has more power over the order in which he perceives the communication.	(b) The setting is more determining. The programme affects the mental disposition of the viewer who is obliged to watch the commercial under the influence of the sequence before and in expectation of the sequence after.

61

precisely the mode of expression, not the fundamental rules of expression. The special effects of the medium are such that one must introduce them as integral considerations into the system of analysis. One may ask, in the first place, how does the change of medium affect the role of advertising as a mediator between the abstract and the concrete.

The medium is expected to exercise a strong influence on the manner in which the mediation could be expressed. The crucial elements are, as before, the product and the protagonists; but while it is possible in static advertising to 'include' the setting in the user, it becomes rather more difficult to do so in dynamic advertising because the commercial is not a unity but a complex construct of sequences. By the virtue of this fact alone the setting is made sufficiently important to be introduced as an independent element. Finally, the temporal aspect must be added as the counterpart and complement to the spatial dimension in static advertising. Naturally, the auditory and locomotive codes should also be integrated into the general system, but these must be left aside for the time being.

If dynamic advertising as a whole is compared, level for level, with static advertising, then television advertising appears to be less abstract because of its rounded appeal to the senses and its closer proximity to the experience of life. Nevertheless, in a sense, it is more abstract too, as recall is completely dependent on memory. The abstract/concrete schema which was first presented in the last chapter is reintroduced with certain modifications to represent the case of dynamic advertising. (See Figure 3.) The differences between the two systems are clear. The additional complexity is expressed in the fact that the number of elements participating in the system is larger and the possible manner of interaction more complex. However, the basic transformation from the abstract to the concrete, though following a rougher course now, remains intact on every level and in any combination. It will be observed that the double movement from top to bottom and from left to right still parallels the gradual decay of the abstract into the concrete.

The temporal dimension is of course crucial. The game of time is played on multiple levels of which the most important is the distinction between 'real time' and 'advertising time'. Real time may last anything between ten seconds and one minute

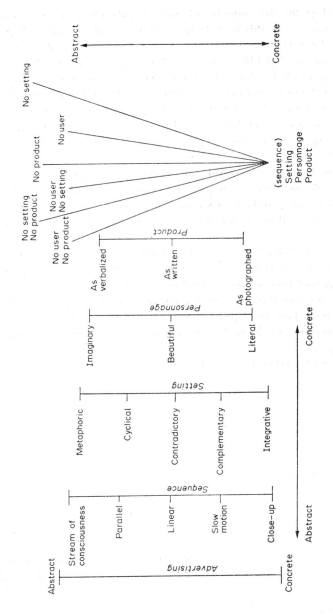

Fig. 3. Dynamic advertising as a mediator between the abstract and the concrete

63

(incidentally, the majority of commercials are shorter than one minute), but in this incredibly short span of time a whole history may be told: boy meets girl, a tragic situation and its happy ending, marital bliss, and so on! It might be concluded, then, that not only is advertising a rhetorical art, the art of the feigned word, but also the art of condensation. No other image says so much in so little. This is, of course, not the only temporal distinction employed by advertising; the game of time is in the essence of the medium and the possibilities are many as depicted in Figure 3.

To illustrate the complexity of the dynamic system, I deliberately chose a very simple example, where only three dimensions are employed and only two points, the polar ones, are considered on each of these scales. The three dimensions are: the Product, the Personage and the Setting. Each of these involve a number of possibilities (Figure 3). For instance, the personage can be totally imaginary, of 'beautiful' people—the ones we should want to resemble—or quite simply 'real' people who in the final analysis are the ones at whom the majority of products are directed. For simplicity's sake only the two extreme points—the imaginary and the real in this example—are selected on each one of the three scales. Adhering to this simple framework, the reference matrix is the following:

		Abstract (a)	Concrete (c)
Setting	$= S$	Metaphoric	Integrative
Personnage	$= U$	Imaginary	Literal
Product	$= P$	Verbalized	Photographed

Since the order of the relations between the elements does not matter, the number of different ways in which it is possible to group the three elements is seven. For instance, a combination Product (P)/Personnage (U)/Setting (S), equals $S/U/P$ or any other possible arrangement. The number of realistic possibilities and the manner in which they can combine, starting from the most abstract and ending with the most concrete, is the following:

$$S$$
$$U$$
$$P$$
$$US$$
$$PS$$
$$PU$$
$$PUS$$

However, in these arrangements the elements are considered as if they each have only one value. In order to take into account the two polar values, the most abstract and the most concrete, of each one of the variables, each possibility must be individually examined. Starting from the last case, it is clear that the total number of eligible combinations is 8 (2^3), which can be arranged in a declining order from the most abstract to the most concrete:

$$P_a\, U_a\, S_a$$
$$P_a\, U_a\, S_c$$
$$P_c\, U_a\, S_a$$
$$P_a\, U_c\, S_a$$
$$P_c\, U_a\, S_c$$
$$P_a\, U_c\, S_c$$
$$P_c\, U_c\, S_a$$
$$P_c\, U_c\, S_c$$

The graded arrangement from the more abstract to the more concrete should not at this stage be taken too rigidly. Some combinations could change place, and whether they do or not depends on the feasibility of measuring the relative degrees of abstractness or concreteness of each combination qua combination. Only then will it be possible to determine unequivocally the order of the possibilities. There is, however, one implicit assumption which may serve as a partial guide in the search for order and which views the relations between the variables in terms of abstractness as $S>U>P$. That is, the setting alone is more abstract than the personage alone, which are in their turn more abstract than an actual picture of the product. Yet it is precisely because I am not concerned with individual elements but with combinations of elements that this relation does not solve the problem for $P_c U_a S_a$ and $P_a U_c S_a$ on the one hand, and $P_c U_a S_c$ and

$P_a U_c S_c$ on the other hand, where the relative degree to which they belong depends most acutely, not on the individual elements, but on the nature of the combination itself. Precisely for this reason the other possibilities are simpler. The PU combinations are 4 (2^2):

$$P_a U_a$$
$$P_a U_c$$
$$P_c U_a$$
$$P_c U_c$$

Similarly the various permutations of the other possibilities could be summarized, giving a totality of twenty-six lawful combinations according to the rules of this game.

2^3	2^2	2^2	2^2	2^1	2^1	2^1	Abstract
$P_a U_a S_a$	$P_a U_a$	$P_a S_a$	$U_a S_a$	P_a	U_a	S_a	
$P_a U_a S_c$	$P_a U_c$	$P_a S_c$	$U_a S_c$	P_c	U_c	S_c	Concrete | Abstract
$P_c U_a S_a$	$P_c U_a$	$P_c S_a$	$U_c S_a$				
$P_a U_c S_a$	$P_c U_c$	$P_c S_c$	$U_c S_c$				
$P_c U_a S_c$							
$P_a U_c S_c$							
$P_c U_c S_a$							Concrete
$P_c U_c S_c$							

While all the combinations are permissible some of them are extremely unlikely to occur (e.g., S_a, S_c, U_a, U_c, $U_a S_a$, $U_a S_c$ and even $U_c S_a$ and $U_c S_c$). The universe of possibilities can be further delimited by ruling out all those which are unlikely to appear for various reasons, and by leaving in the system only those which are practically realizable.

I am now in a position to answer the original question concerning the differences between static and dynamic advertising, and the answer may be given in terms of this table of permutations.

In the static case each one of these possibilities (if I were to separate the protagonists from the setting) would have been, at a single moment of time and for each advertisement, unique; each static image could 'use up' only one alternative at a time. In the dynamic case, the situation is vastly different because each commercial calls upon many possibilities. The inherent flux of sequences enormously increases the modest twenty-six possibilities (which, one may remember, are the simplest case). Even in a short commercial where, say, only five separate sequences are juxtaposed, or superimposed, this moderate stipulation results in 65,780 possibilities.* I concerned myself with these observations in order to render the obvious statement from which I started somewhat more tangible. Cinematic systems are indeed more complex than typographic ones and it is the temporal dimension and not the auditory one which is at the core of this fundamental change.

Nothing has been said so far about the different codes which are employed by the two media. Clearly a system of combinations could be constructed in which the visual and the written codes will represent the static case, and where the dynamic case will be represented by the previous two, as well as by the auditory, the verbal and the locomotive codes. Though this may prove a fascinating exercise, I must stop here to consider the ways in which dynamic advertising lends itself to structural analysis of the type envisaged in the preceding chapter.

Advertising, it might be remembered, is considered to be an intermediate mechanism between symbolic systems and routine consumption behaviour. The object of the analysis is to draw certain conclusions regarding the way in which symbolic systems exert influence on behaviour in the market place. To attempt to do this properly, and in view of the complexity of the deciphering process and the amount of information required for each decoding, the number of product areas I could investigate had to be limited. I finally chose to concentrate on six universal campaigns (where each could be further broken down into smaller campaigns) lasting for about four years each. The total number of commercials analysed is 257 against 124 static advertisements. In spite of the

---

* This figure is calculated on the basis of the combinatorial formula:

$$C^{26}_5 = \frac{26!}{5! \cdot 21!}$$

rather long period of time covered by these campaigns, the commercials in each campaign belong to the same synchronic system, first because they are all different versions presenting essentially one product, and second because commercials are not necessarily restricted to their initial period of creation, but may be transmitted on different occasions with rather long lapses of time between them.

The main characteristics of the products are, as before, completely devoid of any dramatic value. They are 'normal', standardized, mass-produced, routine, repetitive and low expenditure goods. The reason for selecting this type of product is my wish to explore the influence of symbols in the most mundane everyday-life situations. Also, given the character of these products, it is reasonable to assume that the real product differentials are marginal, and that from the point of view of price, availability, convenience and so on, they closely resemble each other. It is thus clear that the only truly variable factor in their market mix is advertising. Therefore, understanding the image of the product and particularly its message is essential to the correct interpretation of the consumption process. Of the six campaigns analysed only four are presented in detail for reasons which will be elaborated in Chapter 6.

Good : evil $\simeq$ powder A : powder B

I will begin as I did in the previous chapter with a relatively simple case, that of a competition between two brands, and proceed from there to an analysis of single universal campaigns.

When the object of study is the whole universe of advertisements telling the complete and detailed story of one *product* field, the problem of individual competition between the specific brands in this product field does not arise. The product campaign as distinct from an individual brand campaign conveys a message which is over and above the peculiarities of any specific brand.

However, when the study is confined to the local war of two brands, the strategic assault staged by them could never be expressed in simple, straightforward binary oppositions. When two competing brands are analysed separately, then the binary oppositions of each are implied in each one of the campaigns, but can never be found in the counter-attack launched by the competitor. The reasons are simple. Two brands can fight each other either by each maintaining that certain attributes are all its own and none characterize the other; or they may both pursue the same line of reasoning, each striving to surpass the other. In either case, when they are both taken as one system, the most extreme claim made will belong to the graded analogue type: a brand will claim to be better than others which do not have to be necessarily bad but merely good. It is the nature of advertising to emphasize the advantages rather than the disadvantages of the product, and both brands insist on advocating their own benefits in comparison with each other. The game becomes not one between pairs of oppository discrete values, or between absolutes, but one in which the comparative and the superlative dominate the scene. As a result a complete multi-brand campaign may resolve into a binary formula, while any two members of the set fail to establish this relation.

Is this fact indeed so strange, or is it in perfect harmony with structuralist theory? Two members of a system do not make a whole; they are merely two members of a much larger system. And in spite of the tempting advocacy of common sense to perceive in two competing brands a pair of binary oppositions, the structuralist non-sense refuses to recognize this as true. It is only as an exhaustive expression of the whole system that the binary formula transpires, not as a private structural arrangement of parts of the system.

There is, of course, a sense in which the analogous comparison may be claimed to be translatable into a digital model as a way of simplifying the resolution. A situation is conceivable where, having formulated comparative codes on a graded scale, the viewer perceives the situation in the following manner: brand A is better than brand B, therefore brand A is good and brand B is bad. However, I do not feel that this solution, though appealing in some respects, is a satisfactory one, be it only for the reasons outlined in Chapter 2—that absolutes of this type are illusory. They are illusory for they are felt to be oppository only because an implicit comparative dimension which gives them this reality can be shown to exist. The system as a whole has a reality which is beyond any individual relations between two brands, and the effectiveness of any particular campaign is determined by its degree of proximity to the overall structural resolution of theme of the system.

The products are simply referred to as washing powder A and washing powder B. The single most insistent distinction between the two brands campaigns is:

brightness vs. whiteness

By no means could these two elements be conceived of on the simple logical level as binary oppositions. Yet is it impossible to prove that one campaign comes closer to the overall fundamental structure than the other and therefore proves more successful? Let us probe behind the scenes and take a look at the reality which manifests itself there.

Powder A advocates brightness. Bright is, in the words of a commercial, more than white—'it doesn't stop at clean and white, it goes on to boost white through to bright.' White, according to brand A, is 'dull'. The relations between the main claims of the two competitors, from the point of view of competitor A, are:

$$\text{white} + \text{clean} = \text{dull}$$
$$\text{bright} > \text{white} \rightarrow \text{powder A} > \text{powder B}$$

From powder B on the other hand, there is no reaction. It is whiteness which is always emphasized and no reference is made to brightness.

But advertisements never advocate a product in isolation, they also propagate a way of living. It is at this point that the real differences between bright and white start to emerge. The different worlds depicted by the commercials are made analogous to the advertised products. Thus product A is 'a bright new power' and product B is 'new energy B washes much whiter'. That this analogy should be drawn is made absolutely certain by the campaign: the powder is 'bright new power for a bright new world'. If the powder must equal the world in which it is expected to take action, then its character is that of the world it serves. The equality may be formed:

$$\text{powder's character} = \text{world's character}$$

It is this equation which puts one on the correct road to the truth, for if it is agreed that this similarity between powder and world exists, then by the simple law of transitivity the characterization of the world reflects the nature of the product too. The 'bright new world' is as the campaign proclaims:

bright new world = tougher
                = more demanding
                = faster
                = hopeless (she feels she would never finish
                   the housework)
                = mechanical
                = enslaving

It is also a world of perspiration, sweat, blood and stains, 'the most difficult even to talk about'—the understains. In short, the bright world is hard, brisk, bullying and ugly.

The wife is depicted as a slave. In a long series of parallel sequences, while the housewife cleans and washes, the family through play, work, negligence and inconsideration, dirties, smears, smudges and smutches. The housewife is invariably the purifying cleansing agent, while the rest of the family are the polluting, contaminating agents. At the end of the weekly ordeal, the commercials offer, if not a solution, at least a reward in the form of a happy family outing. Yet, even there in the reward itself, which is the only scene in which all members of the family are united and in which no division of roles exists, the seeds of the next trial are already sown. The reasons for this are made very clear in the campaign. The reward is contingent upon the ordeal in a vicious circle of cause and effect. In the same manner that the happy outing is dependent upon the weekly chores, the latter have already begun in the midst and as a result of the former. The reward is always but a brief pause between two trials. The division of labour discussed above between the one who cleans and the one who dirties is a glaring reality dwelt upon by the commercials. There is no doubt, though, that it is not the intention of the advertiser to paint a picture of servitude but merely to describe a common situation in a realistic way and in a manner which accords his powder an important role. From the point of view of the consumer, however, the perception of the message could be vastly different. To her, the figure depicted is not a faithful mirror image of herself but a reflection of a slave.

71

The world of brand B is vastly different. It is said to be quiet and white, a world of harmony, where an old-fashioned proud housewife, *la mère de famille*, presides over her family. Behind the rough characterization of working-class *mater familias* peers a happy matriarchy. It is a world where the powder gives 'whiteness', 'extra whiteness', 'new whiteness', 'true whiteness', 'blue whiteness'; where the whiteness one gets is 'as good as gold'. And, of course, the powder itself is blue like the sky, which is a successful colour for detergents of all kinds.

In summary, powder A is tough and powerful; it is a rough powder designed to fight, 'beat' and shoot (for it has a power trigger) enemies dead in a world which is itself unkind. Powder B on the other hand has merely a new energy; it is the same old product but with a new improved formula, which gives it almost 'three times more power to drive out stains'.*

Following the equality drawn before between powder and world, it may be concluded at this stage that whiteness, like brand B, is the symbol of good; and brightness, like brand A, comes closer to exorcizing the spirit of evil. So in spite of the manifest claim in campaign A that brightness *is* more than whiteness, in the perception of the situation the old saying prevails that all that glisters (= brand A) is not gold (= brand B, actually proclaimed in the commercial). This conclusion is not supported just by the description of the world, the designation of the product, the division of labour and the position of the woman in the family, but also in the very framework in which the commercial is situated. Powder A is devoted to the simple, everyday activities of life, play, work, housework, which results in 'the stains one gets simply from living'. The images of powder B are differently constructed. They revolve around three pivots: the interview situation, the demonstration and the swap encounter.

The anonymous street interview is thought to be a particularly frank expression of the truth. The interviewed are chosen at random and remain nameless. In the same sudden fashion that they are cut off from their background and normal surroundings to be put for a brief moment in the limelight of publicity, so they quietly return to their unknown lives. The interview is a

* Incidentally, and I record this only as a curious coincidence, the market share of brand B is almost three times as large as that of brand A (14%/5% = 2·8 times).

sudden confrontation with a question to which the only reply can be open and frank. It is a manner of presenting 'tangible proof' of the many different people who independently of each other have come to the realization of the same truth. As in news or documentary programmes, an authentic portrayal of the truth always resorts to a field interview. To the person staying at home engrossed in an armchair mobility, it offers the opportunity to be transferred, as if by magic, to the scene of the occurrence and to hear the truth from a 'first-hand' source. So, as a first confrontation it allows one to watch what others think and do.

The second technique, the demonstration, involves a test. Will the powder perform the miracle of removing the unshiftable stains or will it fail to achieve this promise? Typically, the test is based on a comparison between the situation before and the situation after the application of the product. Alternatively, and this is a variation on the same idea, a piece of cloth is torn in two: one is washed in powder B and the other in powder X. Invariably, in the nature of such objective scientific tests, the outcome is always in favour of the advertised brand. The personnel carrying out these experiments are typically dressed in white gowns, which not only emphasizes the idea of whiteness but also conjures up the medical profession and the laboratory atmosphere. This atmosphere is further strengthened by the nature of the operation (the test) taking place.

The last situation and the most interesting one is also a test, but this time, the objectivity, the scientific aura has disappeared and in its place a temptation is presented: the single packet the shopper bought will be exchanged for two giant packets of another brand. The temptation it will be realized is that of greed.

The three situations mark a progression from the less extreme to the extreme. The first situation seeks to establish credibility and confidence in the brand in a manner in which the viewer observes the situation as it were from the outside. No judgement is passed, only other people's views and experiences with the product are recorded. The demonstration involves a test, a test of the product by a suspicious consumer, which results in a successful accomplishment of the mission of whiteness 'without a shadow or a stain'. It is then that the approach completely changes and the testing of the product is transformed into the testing of the consumer: will she or will she not succumb to greed? In proclaiming her loyalty to the brand by refusing to swap she in fact demonstrates her immunity to temptation and her flawless moral integrity. She is doing something else too. She proves her loyalty to purity and whiteness and her rejection of temptation and glitter. After all, understood metaphorically, the powder she is faithful to has 'almost three times more power to drive out stains'. There is no need to pursue the religious imagery which uses stains as a constant metaphor for sins. The important point, however, is that powder B is not only a symbol of purity and 'good' against 'evil', but it also projects an absolving power, the power of the priest.

The same conclusion is persistently hammered in if one deviates for a moment from the boundaries of these two campaigns to regard the more general situation in the universe of washing-powder tales. Two facts are of immediate importance: detergents are advertised heavily—it came second only to chocolate confectionery in 1971. It is also, in vast contrast to sweets, the most resented type of all advertising. The resentment has often been attributed to the frequency of exposure, but as sweets are advertised more heavily than detergents, this explanation is not very convincing. Finally, of the twelve brands on the market, nine advocate whiteness as their major feature and the best campaign to date of any washing powder, was the one for Persil whose famous slogan ran: 'Persil washes whiter and whiter, and whiter'. Obviously, there is no logical sense in this declaration and none should be looked for. And yet its success was phenomenal, so much so that this slogan and that campaign are considered to be a classic of the advertising world. But if detergent advertising draws an analogy between washing powders and good and evil and if, moreover, the washing powder is accorded the role of the purifying agent then perhaps it is not very surprising that it is resented so much in an age which has come to look at this type of preaching with a hostile eye. Nevertheless, and this is crucial, it is precisely this type of advertising which is also the most effective, for the ghosts of good and evil are still one of the most potent images of the cultural and religious life of contemporary secular society.

Had I chosen different brands, the definition of the structure

74

could have been sharper; but this is immaterial. The knowledge one has of other brands in this product area strongly indicates that if a similar procedure to the one carried out with baby foods were to be utilized, then the overall resolution for the product campaign would have resulted in an Exhaustive Common Denominator of the type:

good : evil $\simeq$ washing powders : not washing powders

In terms of the viewer's perception the whole campaign projects one fundamental symbol. Within the whole system, the relative efficacy of each individual brand campaign is determined by the relative degree of proximity in which it relates to the overall resolution of theme. The closer it comes to that model, the more likely it is to win. In the totality of relations making up the whole system, brand A is further away from the 'target' than brand B, which never deviates from it. This explains why in the two examples examined here the consistent claim of brand B to whiteness is unerring, and why in spite of the greater sophistication, versatility and creativity of brand A, its performance is rather poor. In failing to agree with the Exhaustive Common Denominator of the system it condemns itself to be identified with the signifier of the 'not washing powders', which is Evil.

Brand R (BR)

This section is devoted to the case of brand R. This brand was the first of its kind on the market and consequently enjoyed for a relatively long time a state of unchallenged supremacy. Later when competitive brands entered the market, the standards established were those of brand R. Thus it is the first case considered by me in which a brand has overlapped for a number of years the whole product area, and therefore the advertisements designed for this special brand amount in fact to the whole universe of tales. Without wishing to anticipate the results, it may be hinted that from the structural point of view this campaign has the closest affinity with universal multi-brand advertising for reasons which will be further elaborated in Chapter 6.

The universal campaign is broken down into sub-sets which are denoted as $S_i = \{S_1, S_2, \ldots, S_n\}(i = 1, 2, \ldots, n)$. Each commercial in the sub-set is denoted as $C_j = \{C_1, C_2, \ldots, C_m\}(j = 1, 2, \ldots, m)$.

75

A notation S_1C_1 means 'commercial one in sub-set one' and so on. The sub-sets and their commercials are given in Appendix III.

Following my usual practice one may begin at any point of the campaign, which happens to be in this case S_1C_1. In this commercial the children are put to bed and the parents are having a romantic dinner for two, which consists of brand R. This dinner is interrupted by the children waking up and demanding attention. The binary set of this single advertisement reads as follows:

brand R : not brand R $\simeq$ romantic dinner : looking after $\simeq$
for two the family
$\simeq$ something special : the routine $\simeq$
$\simeq$ a touch of : ordinary
Indian magic every day life

On the basis of the very limited information which is contained in this single commercial it is already possible to reduce the two sides of the formulae into two exhaustive elements, the unusual against the usual. However, before doing that it may be interesting to inspect the way in which the same theme is further elaborated in the other commercials which belong to the same sub-set. Commercial two suggests a new and special way for the newly married wife to show her love for her husband. The S_1C_2 binary relations are formed among the following elements:

BR : not BR $\simeq$ married three weeks : married a long time $\simeq$
$\simeq$ new and special : ordinary $\simeq$
$\simeq$ love : hate

It will be observed that in this second manifestation one element is already redundant while the other two bits of information are new. Nevertheless the new pairs are reducible to the same exhaustive elements as before. In spite of a certain escalation and the multiple aspects introduced, the fundamental resolution of theme remains unchanged. It is this inclination which is most sharply illustrated in S_1C_3 where the elementary segments achieve their most precise definition. The situation is complex. A man and his wife are having dinner at a friend's place. The husband admires the 'other woman'. To remedy this, the wife is advised to try cooking something different at home. The binary pairs are:

BR : not BR ≃ husband praises : husband does not ≃
                wife's friend   praise wife
       ≃ friend's house   : own house   ≃
       ≃ something special : something usual ≃
       ≃ treated like a   : treated like a
          princess   wife

It is made clear by the commercial that the 'something special' (brand R) transforms the ordinary into the unusual. For the first time it is also explained how it is that this transformation occurs. For, says the commercial, when the wife starts serving brand R the husband is transformed into a prince and the wife into a princess.

When the three sets of expressions are taken together they still retain a certain degree of redundancy. In order to obtain the pure non-repetitive set, the recurrent synonymous elements must be eliminated. The most striking feature of these advertisements is the way in which a limited number of commercials can at times be so sharply defined, that in a unique manifestation the basic structure is already discernible. Once the basic definition is put across, any additional representation serves only to strengthen the point and fortify the initial definition by providing more ammunition for the support of the underlying resolution. The ECD is:

brand R : not brand R ≃ unusual : usual

This fundamental analogy is given to many interpretations because its boundaries are particularly vague and the senses in which it applies particularly rich. It is as if the commercials hesitate among a number of possible underlying themes they can 'choose' to best put their message across. The sense of hesitation is reflected in the fact that the binary expressions lend themselves to several exhaustive reductions. Step by step the recipient is guided to select among the various initial possibilities the one which is best suited to the present campaign. For instance, the food ingredients which are included in the image and which describe the product itself form a homology with the previous binary formulae:

$$\left\{ \begin{array}{l} \text{beef} \\ \text{prawns} \end{array} \right\} : \left\{ \begin{array}{l} \text{soy sauce,} \\ \text{curry sauce} \end{array} \right\} \simeq \left\{ \begin{array}{l} \text{carrots, peas,} \\ \text{mushrooms, onions} \end{array} \right\} : \left\{ \begin{array}{l} \text{Oriental, Chinese} \\ \text{fruits \& vegetables} \end{array} \right\}$$

Though the two sides of the expressions are readily reducible to the usual/unusual in the traditional food consumption in England, one may define them more narrowly at a level which is less abstract, as members of a binary group which are reducible to the native/foreign set.

On the other hand, going back to the first advertisement, S_1C_1, the *jeu de contrastes* between the unusual and the normal verges on the sacred against the profane. (The terms profane and sacred are not used in their religious designation but in their sociological, anthropological sense, in which, according to Edmund Leach, the sacred is equal to the abnormal, special, other worldly, royal, taboo, sick; while the profane equals normal, everyday, of this world, plebeian, permitted, healthy.[5]) The basic movement of the commercial supports this interpretation. It begins with a child being put to bed (=profane), it continues with a dinner for two with a touch of Indian magic (=sacred), and it ends with the children, awakening, calling their parents back to profane reality.

This set of commercials is not restricted to one ECD only but pursues other channels of expression. S_1C_4 minutely follows the development of the relationship between the man and the woman in the commercial. The following pattern emerges:

1. He $\xrightarrow{\text{o}}$ she (No interest: 'He hardly noticed me')

2. Cupid (=BR) ('He took a forkful')

3. He $\xrightarrow{+}$ she ('You were here to stay')

4. He $\xrightarrow[\infty]{+}$ she ('Never look away')

The relations progress from apathy to love, a woman is transformed into a wife and a man into a husband. Brand R itself is depicted in the guise of the divine matchmaker, Cupid, whose arrow is a forkful of BR or in terms of this image the agent of transformation. S_1C_5 portrays the same fundamental movement, but the succession of images is shortened into two quick steps and the transforming agent is only implied.

1. He $\xrightarrow{+}$ she ('It was one of those things, I just looked at
   you . . .')

2. He $\overset{+}{\underset{\infty}{\longrightarrow}}$ she ('Your smile said you were here to stay')

Without S_1C_4 the full meaning of S_1C_5 would have been
harder to decipher. It is only because of this internal game of
the pieces in the jigsaw puzzle, which complement each other
into a meaningful structure, that the process of decoding can
be accomplished. But this is not all. Another element touched
upon before is reintroduced here in a new guise. Let me
return to S_1C_4 where the binary set is arranged in the following
manner:

$$S_1C_4 = \text{all those years ago} \quad : \text{the present} \quad \simeq$$
$$\simeq \text{a woman served brand R} : \text{wife serves brand R} \simeq$$
$$\simeq \text{wife's recollections} \quad : \text{husband's forgetfulness}$$

If to this the binary set of S_1C_6 is immediately added, then:

$$S_1C_6 = \text{past 3} \quad : \text{past 1} \simeq$$
$$\simeq \text{present} : \text{past 1} \simeq$$
$$\simeq \text{past 3} \quad : \text{past 2} \simeq$$
$$\simeq \text{past 1} \quad : \text{the future}$$

where: past 1 = first meeting all those years ago
       past 2 = honeymoon in Venice
       past 3 = tonight's meal
       present = wife's recollections.

The permutations of time create the effect of timeless time, of
time within a time of everlasting time. If it is remembered at this
stage that S_1C_5 explores part of this temporal movement by
suggesting a triple-time typology:

1. First time = past   ('All those years ago')
2. Now   = present ('We have (brand R) a lot now')
3. Forever   = future ('You were here to stay forever')

then, it becomes possible to conclude that the second ECD is one which draws the analogy:

eternal time : profane time $\simeq$ brand R : not brand R

Finally, S_1C_7 draws a picture in which the participating elements are:

$S_1C_7 =$ morning   : evening $\simeq$
       $\simeq$ wife without husband   : wife with husband $\simeq$
       $\simeq$ husband out of the house : husband in the house $\simeq$
       $\simeq$ wedding day   : anniversary

The decoding is only possible in terms of space and in terms of the physical proximity between husband and wife. The following description may help explain what I mean:

morning   ——————→ out (husband and children)/in (wife)
evening   ——————→ in   (husband and wife)
wedding   ——————→ out (husband and wife)
anniversary ——————→ in   (husband and wife)

Interpreted in this manner the process of reduction results in:

in : out $\simeq$ brand R : not brand R

Summarizing the argument so far, it will be realized that three ECDs dominate the scene, the unusual/usual, eternal time/profane time and the in/out. This same conclusion is conveyed by two other commercials, S_1C_5 and S_1C_6. Their binary sets are arranged in a manner which is not easily reducible without the clues provided by the other members of the set. There are too many alternative solutions. The true function and the real significance of these oppositions penetrate through because one is already aware of the total system and the structural resolutions that underlies it. S_1C_6 proceeds to unfold the following pattern:

$S_1C_6 =$ a woman   : wife $\simeq$
       $\simeq$ restaurant   : home $\simeq$
       $\simeq$ foreign country : own country

and S_1C_5:

$S_1C_5 =$ past   : present $\simeq$
       $\simeq$ restaurant   : home $\simeq$
       $\simeq$ waiter serves   : wife serves

Decoding these statements they give a perfect summary of the three ECDs, utilizing (particularly S_1C_5) all the dimensions employed so far. The whole set, which comprises seven commercials, reiterates the fundamental themes in such a way that each commercial offers one part (or more) which is then seized upon by the other commercials and further defined and elaborated till the message is crystal clear. Summarizing this process the following matrix is obtained.

Commercials	Unusual/ usual	In/out	Eternal time/ profane time
S_1C_1	+		
S_1C_2	+		
S_1C_3	+	+	
S_1C_4			+
S_1C_5	+	+	+
S_1C_6	+	+	+
S_1C_7		+	

It is clear from this table that the most dominant and persisting ECD so far is the one which explores the many possibilities inherent in the opposition between the unusual and the usual. It is suggested that the same theme, though more narrowly defined, is investigated by other commercials in the universal campaign and therefore, by branching out in this manner and offering a lever for other images, it constitutes the link which ties sub-set S_1 to the rest of the commercials in their diverse manifestations. Thus S_2C_{1-3} maintain:

S_2C_{1-3} = Italian   : Englishman $\simeq$
       $\simeq$ Chinaman   : Englishman $\simeq$
       $\simeq$ Indian   : Englishman $\simeq$
       $\simeq$ the insider   : the outsider $\simeq$

$\simeq$ home and family   : street $\simeq$
$\simeq$ mama's cooking   : wife's cooking $\simeq$
$\simeq$ happiness   : sadness

And the ECD is:

the endogenous : the exogenous $\simeq$ brand R : not brand R

Brand R becomes a symbol of *des nôtres*, mama, an image of identification of our kind against their kind. But in this case the cards change hands twice. To the viewer, it is they, the dramatis personae, the people in the commercials—the Indian, the Italian and the Chinese—who are the outsiders. And yet in the commercial it is the insider—the Englishman—who is depicted as an outsider. And in real life it is not they, the strangers, who invite him to join them in their milieu (as they do in the commercial), but the insider who admits them into his domain through the consumption of brand R. Thus, there is a native viewer who is labelled foreign and there are also foreign personae who behave as if they were natives and who are prepared to admit into their midst a foreigner who is in fact a non-foreigner.

In real life, however, the situation is diametrically opposed, for the stranger of the commercial is the native of the land, and the insiders of the advertisements are the outsiders in life. It is thus that the message is doubly inverted in the viewer's mind and it is in this manner that he is reconciled to the admittance of the other kind into his kind, i.e., by consuming foreign foods. It will be noticed too, that the other dimension employed in the previous set, the in against the out, also recurs here not only figuratively but also physically in the form of the street against home.

Let us move on now to the next sub-campaign which pursues a thread that another campaign has started to weave and which also adds a new dimension. The binary set of S_3C_{1-6} is:

brand R : not brand R $\simeq$ joy   : not joy $\simeq$
                    $\simeq$ love   : not love $\simeq$
                    $\simeq$ happy wife   : sad wife $\simeq$
                    $\simeq$ approving   : disapproving
                        husband   husband $\simeq$
                      $\simeq$ marital bliss   : marital failure $\simeq$
                      $\simeq$ sophisticated meal : plain meal

Where the process of reduction results in the ECD:

$$\text{happiness : misery} \simeq \text{brand R : not brand R}$$

Love is introduced as one of the food ingredients making up the dish; it becomes an integral part of the meal. The food ingredients themselves introduce the second dimension, the endogenous/exogenous, with love unerringly always on the endogenous side in the following manner:

$$
\begin{array}{lll}
S_3 C_{1\text{-}6} = \text{beef} & : \text{rice} & \simeq \\
\simeq \text{love} & : \text{curry} & \simeq \\
\simeq \text{soft noodles} & : \text{soy sauce} & \simeq \\
\simeq \text{love} & : \text{crispy noodles} & \simeq \\
\simeq \text{beef} & : \text{vegetables} & \simeq \\
\simeq \text{love} & : \text{golden rice} & \simeq \\
\simeq \text{chicken} & : \text{sultanas} & \simeq \\
\simeq \text{love} & : \text{patna rice} \simeq \text{etc.}
\end{array}
$$

By using love as one of the food ingredients a focal point of intersection is established between the two major themes employed. Love symbolizes the 'in' side of the binary pair and it also signifies 'happiness', consequently the consumer of brand R is offered a position on the positive diagonal of love, representing all the possibilities in a two-dimensional world of being both in and happy.

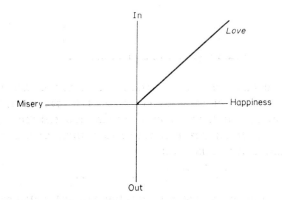

It has been mentioned before that the initial point through which one penetrates the system is immaterial as long as at the end of the journey the analysis is able to circumscribe a complete circle. It is only at this stage that the analysis may be said to have exhausted the system of appearances. The subsequent campaign describes the transformation from culture to nature by using the following elements:

$$S_4 C_{1-3} = (\text{'exotic' woman/'civilized' woman, outdoors splendour/indoors bliss, country/city})$$

Brand R is the link and the agent of transformation between the 'primitive' woman and the 'civilized' woman, between outdoors splendour and indoors bliss and between country life and urban life. The mood is that of a primitive village, of a natural unmarred beauty, of purity and calm, which are bestowed by brand R on its civilized urban consumer. The moment of consumption is said to be made special precisely because in that moment the city consumer is offered a vicarious experience of nature.

The association between the product, the mood and nature is even stronger in $S_4 C_{4-6}$ where the pastoral effects are greatly enhanced. A beautiful, voluptuous exotic woman glides across fields and forests, holding a basket filled with the fruit of the earth. In another commercial the woman sits in a boat which floats gently upon water. Ancient images of fecundity and the all powerful ever longed for *terra mater* are evoked. The binary oppositions employed are:

$$S^5 C^{5-6} = \text{water/earth; village/town; outdoors splendour/indoors bliss; 'exotic' woman/'civilized' woman; floating/walking; boat/car; fertility/sterility}$$

The six commercials taken together reiterate the theme of the return to nature, or alternatively, if it is so preferred, the reintegration of nature in cultural life through the mediation of brand R. It is perhaps permissible then to form the ECD expression in a slightly different manner:

$$\text{brand R: } \{\text{nature} \rightarrow \text{culture}\}$$

Brand R is the agent of integration, the mediator between nature and culture. It will be seen later that the same process is reversed in another campaign for a different product.

84

Finally, brand R exults in an esoteric knowledge, a secret shared with no one. Omnipotent science of magic and the secrets which nature keeps to herself are made accessible to brand R only. It is the wisdom of the 'how' in contrast to the wisdom of the 'what' which is portrayed in S_5C_{1-6}:

brand R : not brand R $\simeq$ novel : ordinary $\simeq$
$\simeq$ singular knowledge : everybody's knowledge $\simeq$
$\simeq$ part : whole $\simeq$
$\simeq$ how : what $\simeq$
$\simeq$ magic hand : human hand

Brand R possesses a unique knowledge of how to create something special out of well known natural ingredients. It is thus that the final two dimensions are related by a double movement. Culture is transformed into nature through the omniscience of brand R: a modern laboratory is able to create and capture that special mood of nature. And simultaneously, nature is transformed into culture in the same way that in the commercials the exotic country woman is transformed into a European city lady, through the consumption of brand R. The internal motion is:

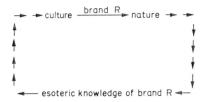

The whole universal campaign—the five sub-sets—is held together by each sub-set throwing a bridge over to the next sub-set with the 'last' sub-set, which is arbitrarily chosen, closing the circle by reaching back to the 'first' sub-set. Without stopping at this stage to draw together all the thematic relations between the various dimensions, it is already clear that a degree of affinity could be established between in/out, and endogenous/exogenous, between nature/culture and eternal time/profane time, and so on. The only comment one permits oneself at this stage is that it is possible, using these affinities, to close the circle and thus establish

H.M.—D

a complete exhaustive picture of the whole universal campaign. Pulling together the dimensions used so far the following pattern emerges:

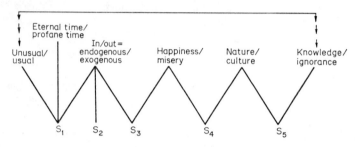

The solid lines show which dimensions are employed in each set and the way in which the sets are tied together through these dimensions. For instance, S_1 utilizes three dimensions while the endogenous/exogenous theme itself is employed in three different sub-sets.

The whole campaign explores through the use of five basic dimensions a number of basic transformations among which the following are the most important:

$$
\begin{aligned}
\text{man} &\longrightarrow \text{husband} \\
\text{woman} &\longrightarrow \text{wife} \\
\text{newly married} &\longrightarrow \text{family} \\
\text{usual} &\longrightarrow \text{unusual} \\
\text{the exogenous} &\longrightarrow \text{the endogenous} \\
\text{past} &\longrightarrow \text{future, eternity} \\
\text{misery} &\longrightarrow \text{happiness} \\
\text{ignorance} &\longrightarrow \text{knowledge} \\
\text{culture} &\longrightarrow \text{nature}
\end{aligned}
$$

By a constant game of permutations, the basic dimensions interact with each other and cross one another at certain points of intersection. By so doing they reconstruct a network of relations which lends the system its versatility and creativity.

Simultaneously, they endow the system with the power to put across the fundamental message.

Brand E (BE)

This analysis is devoted to a single campaign for frozen vegetables.

The actual products advertised differ: they may be frozen potatoes, peas, beans, sprouts or mixed vegetables. These differences are unimportant. The whole campaign is regarded as one system in which the participating elements are relevant only in so far as they establish significant relations among themselves. The specific products advocated within the general system of frozen vegetables are immaterial because, at the very least, some of them—the green vegetables—can be easily substituted for each other in the commercials without causing great differences in consumer perception. Indeed, this fact has been recognized by the advertiser himself who often uses very similar theme advertising for the various types of vegetables, which nevertheless constitute one system. Some advertisements are almost identical on the surface level, so much so that they can be regarded as one basic advertisement to which some trimmings—the different vegetables—are added. This is particularly true when the same copy is used with different themes or the same theme is used with different copies. Both have the effect of exploring different variations of the same motif.

Let us turn now to the campaign itself. In S_1C_1 an old country woman is shown growing vegetables. She chooses the perfect and rejects the imperfect. She has been doing this all her life till she discovered brand E whereupon she stopped growing her own vegetables and started to buy brand E. In S_1C_2, on the other hand, a huge question mark is shot on the screen and the question is asked: what makes 'a good meal memorable'? Of course it is brand E which makes it memorable, but more importantly the two seemingly unrelated commercials unfold a state of perfect opposition to one another.

S_1C_1 :	country woman	single	old	at work
S_1C_2 :	city folk	couples	young	on holiday

	S_1C_1 :	producer	the rejected
	S_1C_2 :	consumer	the chosen

S_1C_1 goes on to explore the relationships between the old country woman and brand E. While the old woman chooses the perfect, brand E chooses the perfect at their best, and while she picks the perfect throughout a period of a few short weeks in the year, brand E chooses them on the very day they are at their best. Thus, brand E is to the old woman like the best is to the better. While she does much better than others, brand E does the very best. The relations are not digital but comparative. The two elements are compared to each other not in terms of some absolutes, but in terms of their relative performance. If the comparison is one of skills, then her activities are particularly important. These consist of rejecting the stringy in preference for the tender and choosing the perfect rather than the rubbery and skinny. Reducing the series mentioned so far, the ECD, through the analogy between the country woman and brand E, is:

$$\text{the chosen : the rejected} \simeq \text{brand E : not brand E}$$

This fundamental theme constitutes a further bond between the two commercials beyond the purely formal fact that they are positioned in perfect opposition to each other. The producer rejects the imperfect thus allowing the consumer the benefit of 'the perfect at their best'. It is precisely this fact which makes the meal in S_1C_2 memorable.

The next sub-set discloses a different situation. One is no longer with the producer and the consumer but instead one is asked to witness an encounter between a street greengrocer and a shopper in an outdoors market-place. It will be immediately recognized that the previous more extreme opposition between producing and consuming is restated now in a mitigated form. The producer, one may say the grower, is transformed into a greengrocer, and final consumption, eating, is transformed into a shopping expedition, thus:

grower

greengrocer

shopper

final consumer

In the past farmers used to sell their produce in the market-place. The street greengrocer is a close reminder of that situation, but the 'distance' between this function and final consumption has already degenerated into a less abstract level. For the greengrocer is not a farmer any longer but an intermediary consumer as well as a seller, and the shopper is a consumer and a 'seller' too because she still needs to 'sell' the product to the final consumer, her family. In this sense the greengrocer is a mediator between the producer and the shopper, and the shopper is a mediator between the greengrocer and the final consumer.

In the same commercials the grocer is unable to accommodate the shopper because the vegetables she demands are out of season. At this point a brand E delivery truck appears with a fresh stock of the unavailable vegetables, whereupon the shopper leaves the greengrocer to buy in the supermarket. Under these conditions the delivery car refutes the tie between the shopper and the greengrocer and instead establishes a new connexion between shopper and producer via the supermarket, 'the BE shop'. Stringing all the pieces together the previous diagram may be completed in the following manner:

```
           grower
                     producer
                     greengrocer        supermarket
                                        housewife
                     shopper
                                        the family
    final consumer
```

The two extreme oppositions—grower/final consumer—deteriorate into a softer contrast between producer and shopper. The grocer becomes the mediator between the two. The second triad is then re-expressed on a lower level of abstraction. The producer disappears altogether and the grocer/shopper opposition is put across in yet a different way: the supermarket/housewife + family relation. The shopper of the second triad becomes the mediator between the housewife and the family of the last triad. In this way the whole series of commercials are held together. The basic opposition is reiterated in different forms through a process of mediation and growing concretization in a persistent attempt to get through to the viewer.

The delivery van becomes the vehicle of transportation, not only from the grower to the shop but also from S_1C_{1-2} to the following sub-set, S_2C_{1-4}. The internal transformations continue to pursue a course of declining extremity and decaying contrast.

S_2C_{1-4} explore other possibilities too. The binary set may be summarized in the following way:

brand E : not brand E $\simeq$ in season   : out of season $\simeq$
         $\simeq$ indoors   : outdoors $\simeq$
         $\simeq$ supermarket   : market-place $\simeq$
         $\simeq$ modern delivery : old cart $\simeq$
           van

Reducing these expressions to their Exhaustive Common Denominator, the conclusion reached is:

in : out $\simeq$ brand E : not brand E

This fundamental opposition is explored by the binary set above, from two points of view: seasonality and various manifestations of physical interiority against exteriority.

The producer-consumer theme is taken up again in the most persistent advertising sub-campaign of brand E. Invariably, the commercials unfold a complete cycle between the farmer, the original gardener, and the final consumer, the family.

The system of appearances, however, does not stop at that, for the farmer's land is also identified with home and country, so:

brand E : not brand E $\simeq$ brand E country   : other $\simeq$
         $\simeq$ the country (England) : abroad $\simeq$
         $\simeq$ home   : exile

Moreover, brand E comes from brand E country which is at once home- and mother-land. In unfolding their meaning the commercials clearly emphasize this aspect: the vegetables are consumed at home by a mother and her children or by the children alone. No man ever takes part in this ritual and the children are paralleled, indeed identified with the product; thus, the children of the house and the produce of the land are one and the same. The old country woman is transformed into a young modern housewife whose children are, like the perfect product, small, sweet and tender. No man ever takes part in consuming because in the world created by these commercials the man is cast in the role of the producer. The only link between production and consumption must be through the product itself. The appearance of the grower at the family table could have thrown these categories into confusion. It will be realized that the ECD is:

the endogenous : the exogenous $\simeq$ brand E : not brand E

which is, like in the case of brand R, but another way of expressing the previous distinction between the in and the out, our kind against their kind.

The complex of the non-verbal code describes typical country scenes, endless fields, early morning sunrise, splendid isolation, silence and tranquillity, simple joys and quiet happiness, but above all else a close proximity to nature. The fields are never violated with modern brutal machinery. They are slowly and gently furrowed by an ancient primitive plough pulled by horses. It is not only natural authenticity that the advertisements wish to convey but also the idea that the changeless, unviolated original purity of the land is preserved intact in brand E country. The primitive plough itself is a cosmic symbol of an extremely wide currency. It was and still is regarded in some places as a gift from the gods intended not only for agricultural purpose but also for religious and ceremonial usage. This primitive plough and horse are transformed in S_2C_{1-4} into the delivery van which establishes, as has been shown before, the vital link between country, earth, and the original farmer on the one hand, and the final consumer on the other. It may also be remembered that in order that the 'city folk' will enjoy their memorable meal they must leave their normal surroundings behind and 'go back' to nature.

Already another crucial theme manifests itself where the ECD reads:

nature : culture $\simeq$ brand E : not brand E

or more specifically in terms of this system:

brand E : {nature→culture}

It is not merely the analogy between the product and nature which is emphasized here but mainly the return to the origins and the bond with the earth.

91

Having firmly set the scene in an original archaic country the images go on to unfold their hidden meaning:

$$S_3C_{5-6} = \text{winter} \qquad\qquad\quad : \text{spring} \qquad\qquad\qquad \simeq$$
$$\simeq \text{land lies sleeping} \qquad : \text{land grows green} \qquad \simeq$$
$$\simeq \text{land lies fallow} \qquad\;\; : \text{land full of goodness} \simeq$$
$$\simeq \text{land covered with mud} : \text{land covered with green}$$

where the usual process of reduction reveals the ECD to be:

$$\text{life : death} \simeq \text{brand E : not brand E}$$

The theme of life and death is further enhanced by an extremely skilful use of specific symbols. The commercials begin with a shot of a bird which flies over the vast expanse of fields till it disappears beyond the horizon. It symbolizes the passage of time between winter and spring and between death and regeneration. The second constant image is very appropriately that of a bridge. The bridge is, in numerous mythologies, the symbol of the crossing between the land of the dead and the land of the living. And even if it is not Cerberus that is the custodian of the bridge, an ordinary dog plays this role perfectly.

If any doubts are still lingering in the viewer's mind, the meaning is made absolutely clear in S_3C_{7-10}:

$$S_3C_{7-10} = \text{silence} \qquad\;\; : \text{noise} \qquad\qquad \simeq$$
$$\simeq \text{asleep} \qquad\quad\; : \text{awake} \qquad\qquad \simeq$$
$$\simeq \text{sleeping sun} : \text{crowing cock} \simeq$$
$$\simeq \text{evening} \qquad\;\; : \text{morning} \qquad\;\; \simeq$$
$$\simeq \text{freezing cold} : \text{fire} \qquad\qquad\;\; \simeq$$
$$\simeq \text{adult man} \quad\;\; : \text{young child}$$

All the elements on the right-hand side are symbols of a new beginning, of genesis, while the elements on the left-hand side are 'sear and yellow leaf' symbols of the twilight of life. To complete the imagery of birth, regeneration and genesis, a gentle hint is addressed to procreation too:

$$S_3C_{11-12} = \text{sun} \qquad\qquad\quad : \text{earth} \qquad\qquad\qquad \simeq$$
$$\simeq \text{boy} \qquad\qquad\; : \text{girl} \qquad\qquad\qquad\;\; \simeq$$
$$\simeq \text{lying in the field} : \text{sitting on a fence} \qquad \simeq$$

$\simeq$ reclining, playing with : walking with a basket $\simeq$
a pod boat
$\simeq$ reaping : growing

The sun and the earth, the great cosmological pair, participate in the process of a universal conception. With typical Freudian imagery, a boy reclining over water rows a boat made of pod in a pond; and the pod, it is said, is filled with perfect little peas. The little girl, on the other hand, collects peas in her basket and consumes them, sitting on a fence. On the content level the innocence of the children is emphasized. They are, like the product, sweet, small and perfect.

In direct contrast to this image of procreation, the spectre of a threat to life is raised. The peas are said to be picked young almost before they are grown, a statement which strongly connotes death. Simultaneously, a small child sitting on horseback is being led in an unknown direction. As the identity of child and product has been emphasized all along, the image evokes rather strongly the scene of the sacrifice. Thus two things are simultaneously accomplished, for to the question of whether the child is being led to death, the inevitable answer is that brand E is destined to play the role of the ram caught in the thicket. The series of oppositions employed are:

$$S_3C_{13} = \text{man/child; leads/led; rough/tender; on foot/}$$
$$\text{on horseback}$$

Thus in a very prolonged series of commercials the themes of life and death, the beginning of life and the beginning of the end, almost life and almost death are explored in a quite ruthless persistence.

One may stop here to summarize the argument so far. A series of transformations are explored. These are:

$$\text{nature} \longrightarrow \text{culture}$$
$$\text{dead season} \longrightarrow \text{fertile season}$$
$$\text{death} \longrightarrow \text{life, genesis}$$

There is, however, one aspect which is left unanswered: all the symbols are those of regeneration and life but the product itself is dead and frozen. Not very surprisingly, perhaps, this aspect is

93

never mentioned in the advertisements themselves. But in order to fight off the potentially negative connotations this fact may have, a convincing counter-claim must be launched. Consequently, an image of hot vibrating warmth is needed. It is precisely this aspect which is scrutinized by S_4C_{1-8} which read:

brand E : not brand E $\simeq$ tempting value   : poor value $\simeq$
                       $\simeq$ attractive   : not attractive $\simeq$
                       $\simeq$ great harvest   : bad harvest $\simeq$
                       $\simeq$ woman delighted : woman horrified $\simeq$
                       $\simeq$ sizzling   : deep freeze

where the process of reduction to the ECD results in:

$$\text{hot : cold} \simeq \text{brand E : not brand E}$$

And if there are still any doubts left, the last commercial in this series puts forward a statement which is quite unequivocal. S_4C_9 uses the same basic oppositions as before; at the same time it indulges in a game of degrees in the following manner:

$$\text{smallest peas} = \text{smaller price}$$
$$\text{sweetest peas} = \text{sweeter price}$$
$$\text{dazzling sun} = \text{price}$$

Adding up the first two equations results in:

$$\text{peas (smallest + sweetest)} = \text{price (smaller + sweeter)}$$

As dazzling sun = price, it is possible to substitute dazzling sun for price in the above equation and obtain the result that brand E (peas) is even more dazzling than the sun, which is, of course, hot.

We may turn now to the last set of commercials left in the campaign and begin with S_5C_1 where the following relations emerge:

$$\text{woman} \xrightarrow{\text{sees}} \text{brand E} \xleftarrow{\text{talks}} \text{man}$$

There is no direct communication between the man and the woman but rapport is nevertheless established through the products of which he talks and which she sees. He tries hard to draw her attention but fails because the products are stronger than he is. The scene is set in a modern supermarket which establishes a point of contact between the commercials in this set and S_2.

S_5C_2 continues in the same vein, but an element of action and a point of communication is finally established. The man tries again to talk to the woman but she does not listen. Nevertheless, she does exactly what he is trying to tell her to do, without seemingly succeeding in getting through to her. Therefore, once a decision has been taken by her, a bridge is thrown over the communication gap and he finally succeeds in establishing contact with her by giving approval to the choice she made. The final movement of the relations is:

$$
\begin{array}{l}
\qquad\text{(a) chooses} \qquad \text{(b) approves} \\
\rightarrow \text{woman} \longrightarrow \text{brand E} \longleftarrow \text{man} \rightarrow \rightarrow \rightarrow \rightarrow \\
\uparrow \qquad\qquad\qquad\qquad\qquad\qquad\qquad\qquad\quad \downarrow \\
\leftarrow \leftarrow \leftarrow \text{(a) tries to attract her attention in vain} \leftarrow \leftarrow \leftarrow
\end{array}
$$

The man's pursuit is hot and urgent trying to provoke her into response, the woman on the other hand, being engrossed in brand E, is cold and unresponsive.

It may be remembered that according to the previous definition the products are hot and as such they are opposites of the woman's coolness. Yet in this scene in the supermarket the products are frozen and the whole encounter takes place across the two sides of the freezing compartment. So in contrast to the previous definition the products are now cold. It is only when communication is finally established through brand E that the products too are unfrozen, for the act of purchase has been accomplished and they are now destined to be cooked. As if to confirm this interpretation the hot aspect of brand E is re-established in three short frying scenes, where no figures appear. Only voices are heard discussing the product, which is meanwhile being fried in a pan. The main contention is:

$$\text{potato fries} > \text{ordinary potatoes}$$

and the reasons given for this are all transformable into the senses, such that:

$$S_6C_{1-3} \equiv \text{round} \qquad\qquad = \text{sight, touch}$$

crinkly	= sight, touch
extra crisp	= touch, sound
fat crisp	= touch
corrugated	= sight, touch
grooves	= sight, touch
fluffy	= touch
lightest	= touch
crunchy	= sound
beautiful things	= sight
fried in pan	= sight, smell
voices only	= sound
broken crockery	= sight, sound

$$S_6C_3 \equiv +\text{a man eats} \qquad = \text{sight}$$

The transformations are directly effected between the attributes and the senses for four of the senses. The exception is the sense of taste. The viewer has to supplement the advertisements here, and by so doing completes them. And this is not all. The system of appearances proceeds to establish a link with the previous campaign by continuing the analogy between a woman and the product, for the product is transformed into an image of a desirable woman and the advice given by the commercial to the viewer is: 'taste that new shape'.

One may stop to summarize here. The Exhaustive Common Denominators employed in the campaign are five:

$$ECD_1 = \text{life } (+\text{genesis, regeneration})/\text{death}$$
$$ECD_2 = \text{hot}/\text{cold}$$
$$ECD_3 = \text{in}/\text{out}$$
$$ECD_4 = \text{original producer}/\text{final consumer}$$
$$ECD_5 = \text{culture}/\text{nature}$$

Nevertheless, in terms of the emphasis and reiteration devoted to these ECDs it is clear that ECD_3 and ECD_5 are relatively less important, and though one would need them in order to build up a transformation diagram as was done in the previous case, their link in the chain is rather weak. ECD_4 is very closely affiliated, one may even say, integrated, with ECD_1, and these two can be considered for all practical purposes as one dimension.

Perhaps a word of explanation is in order here. The division of labour among the three parties—the original producer, the manufacturer and the final consumer—is complex. The original producer is allocated the constructive role of creation (life). The manufacturer is given the violent role of the killer and the processor (death). He is transforming the living thing—animal, bird, fruit or vegetable—into various forms of palatable death. And the consumer is given the thankless role of the carcass-eater, the one who has to feed on death in order to live. This impossible dilemma between the ferocious aspect and the human aspect of societal life, and, moreover, the absolute helplessness of man to solve this inherent contradiction, in which life can be nourished only through death, and in which man can only be either the killer or the vulture, is one of the basic conflicts of human life. The two scales, ECD_1 and ECD_4, are related in this sense.

Let us return to the two major ECDs, ECD_1 and ECD_2. It will be realized that, on the basis of these two dimensions alone, one can summarize all the possible conditions which the product may take.

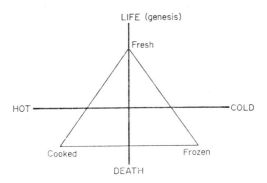

The product can be fresh, frozen, cooked or rotten. When vegetables are fresh they are 'alive' and neither hot nor cold but somewhere in between. When they are cooked they are both dead and hot and when they are frozen they are dead and cold. Depending on the initial point of comparison, rotten could be either cold and death when compared with fresh, or hot and death when compared with frozen.

I have striven to show the intricate ways in which the

97

advertisements in this campaign, and the ones that preceded it, interact to create a complete network of relationships and to reveal their true dimensions in their correct arrangements by reducing the message into the simplest, most precise and most abstract form. In this chapter four major campaigns are surveyed, each throwing light on a different aspect of dynamic advertising and the conclusions one may reach, starting from the structuralist perspective. One may proceed now to examine the possibility of measuring the implications of these findings in terms of their impact on consumption behaviour.

References

1. G. E. Stearn, ed., *McLuhan Hot and Cold* (Penguin Books, 1968); S. Finkelstein, *Sense and Nonsense of McLuhan* (New York: International Publishers, 1968); J. Miller, *McLuhan* (Fontana, 1971).
2. M. McLuhan, *The Mechanical Bride* (Routledge & Kegan Paul, 1951); McLuhan, *The Gutenberg Galaxy* (Routledge & Kegan Paul, 1962); McLuhan, *Understanding Media: The Extension of Man* (New York: McGraw Hill, 1965); McLuhan, *The Medium is the Message* (New York: Bantam Books, 1967); McLuhan, *From Cliché to Archetype* (New York: Pocket Books, 1971).
3. R. Barthes, *Système de la Mode* (Paris: Editions du Seuil, 1967); Barthes, *Elements of Semiology* (Jonathan Cape, 1967); C. Metz, 'Propositions méthodologiques pour l'analyse du film', *Information sur les Sciences Sociales*, vol. 7, No. 4 (August 1968), p. 108; Metz, 'La grande syntagmatique du film narratif', in *Communications*, no. 11 (1966); U. Eco, 'Semiologie des messages visuels', in *Communications*, no. 15 (1970); L. Marin, 'La description de l'image', ibid.
4. A. Martinet, *Elements of General Linguistics* (Faber, 1960).
5. E. R. Leach, 'Magical Hair', *Journal of the Royal Anthropological Institute*, vol. 87 (1957), pp. 147–64.

5. ECDs and their efficacy

It remained unconscious, and so it was active and unconscious at the same time. Freud

This chapter is in some respects a deviation from the general orientation of this work as it tries to apply some well established statistical methods to a problem which probably calls for a special technique. Moreover, this is done with the impatience of the novice at a stage which I am not altogether convinced is not premature.

In the preceding chapters certain fundamental dimensions were shown to underlie the advertising system of appearances. It is hypothesized that the ECDs, though operating on the unconscious level, nevertheless do not escape perception and, moreover, exert influence on consumer behaviour. In this chapter I intend to put this assumption to some preliminary tentative statistical tests—without, however, presuming to do more than scratch the surface of a problem which warrants a separate study in its own right.

This examination is prompted by one basic consideration. My aim is to investigate the way in which symbolic systems are perceived and are brought to bear on everyday consumption behaviour. The answer given so far is not comprehensive, in the sense that it does not apply itself to all the relevant aspects which impinge upon the problem. But then it was never intended that it should do so, and the question of advertising perception is examined from a point of view which hitherto has been neglected.

It is assumed within the framework of this study, that the only changing variable is advertising, and all the other variables affecting consumption behaviour are held constant. This assumption is not as detached from reality as it may seem at first sight. On the contrary, it is particularly realistic in a market where the products are similar in price and quality, where the distribution system remains very much the same over long periods of time, where income changes do not alter consumption habits dramatically and where taste remains constant. Under these circumstances the only truly changing variable in the market-mix is the image of the product or, in other words, advertising in the wider sense of the word. Of course, even within the boundaries of this definition, attention is devoted, in this approach, to one aspect only. Many issues, such as media planning, media schedules, surface message, recall, and so on, are left out. Nevertheless, it is felt that within the terms of reference (i.e., regarding the advertising process as a mechanism of mediation between symbolic systems and everyday behaviour), attention is devoted to the one aspect which is simultaneously most pertinent and yet most neglected. It is because of curiosity, which Aristotle recognizes as the mother of all inquiry, that it was decided to try to see if it is possible to measure the impact of the ECD dimensions on actual behaviour.

The problem itself is a complex one. In the first place, one must test the hypothesis that a correlation exists between the occurrence of certain ECDs and consumer response. Assuming that such a correlation may be shown to exist, the second question, and the more ambitious one, is to examine the possibility of detecting not only a correlation but also a certain direction in the relationship. More particularly, to hold constant all the other economic and marketing variables and investigate the manner in which individual ECDs affect consumer response. In other words, to enquire for any ECD, X, whether it has a positive or a negative effect on the market and the magnitude that this effect may have. These two interrelated problems are investigated in this chapter. Before proceeding, however, a word must be said about some of the difficulties involved.

In the first place, one deals here with a qualitative phenomenon which does not lend itself to direct measurement. Consequently, some indirect measures must be found, which must nevertheless be a satisfactory surrogate. In this case a classification into groups, each controlled by one ECD, was found useful. In other words, all the advertisements which have the same Exhaustive Common Denominator are grouped together. If there are five different ECDs, there will also be five different groups of advertisements. It then becomes possible to measure the effect of each group of advertisements on the actual performance of the product in the market place.

Second, it is the essence of the problem that measurement is relative. In a campaign which is completely governed by one ECD, the conclusions that one may draw about the efficacy of this ECD are extremely limited, for there is no established measure in terms of which it could be assessed and there is no other set without a structural definition or with a different structural definition to which it could be compared. Furthermore, in such cases the problem poses itself in a slightly different manner. One does not wish to measure the relative efficacy of several structural dimensions but rather, in a similar way to the case of brand A and brand B (see pp. 74–75), one wishes to assess the relative distance of any specific realization of the system from the overall ECD of the product system. Unless a scale is established along which every manifestation may be evaluated, there is no possibility of conducting such a test. It follows that the simplest way to approach this question of efficacy, and to test the hypothesis that different ECD dimensions have a distinguishable effect on consumer perception and consequently on consumer response, is by selecting an example in which different dimensions partake.

The general campaign could then be categorized into sub-sets which are governed by different structural resolutions of themes, and the relation between these themes and a measure of consumer response could be established. Because of these considerations one is naturally guided into selecting an example of a universal campaign which is underpinned by different ECDs. As the amount of data required is very extensive and the sources rather limited, only one example is discussed, though the same procedure could have been repeated with any number of products. It must be reiterated that what I am about to attempt is by no means a perfect procedure. I merely try, in order to satisfy my own curiosity, to see whether, using some conventional statistical methods, any light can be shed on this issue. I have no doubt that much more can be accomplished by a method specifically tailored to suit the problem at hand.

First hypothesis: a correlation exists between ECDs and consumer response

The first hypothesis is that the structural resolution of themes influences consumer perception of the product and consequently has an effect on actual behaviour or, more particularly, that a correlation exists between consumer response, as judged by volume sales, and the ECD dimensions.

The brand selected for the purposes of this exposition is brand BR. Previous analysis of the system of appearances revealed five major structural themes:

    (*a*) endogenous/exogenous   (=E/E)
    (*b*) external time/profane time (=ET/PT)
    (*c*) happiness/misery   (=H/M)
    (*d*) knowledge/ignorance   (=K/I)
    (*e*) nature/culture   (=N/C)

How these dimensions are related to each other and in what sense they belong to one system is for the moment immaterial. These issues will be discussed in Chapter 7. The important point to realize is that these dimensions underlie the whole universal campaign of brand BR and that all the commercials making up this general campaign could be reduced to these five dimensions.

The first hypothesis stipulates a connexion between consumer response and these dimensions. Consumer response is measured not by the usual means of perception tests, recall rate and such like, but by the simplest and perhaps the most straightforward measure, that of volume sales. This indicator has been chosen rather than sales value, for instance, in order to avoid the possible effect of inflation. This effect is bound to be expressed in price increase, which in turn is echoed in a sales figure, which does not reflect a genuine rise in demand but only the result of selling the same volume or even a smaller volume for a higher price. As I happen to be interested in real change in demand, volume sales is a more appropriate indicator. There is, of course, another possibility of representing consumer preference, that of changes in the market share of a brand. However, because this specific product is a dominant brand, indeed until a few years ago the only product of its kind, it still enjoys the advantageous position of a market leader, and the change produced in the market share of the product as a result of competitors' activities has not been large enough to fit the purposes of this analysis. It may be emphasized that this by no means implies that there were no changes, but simply that a difference say of 3 per cent between 69 per cent and 72 per cent, while fairly large in terms of sales, is not big enough to be evaluated by the statistical methods used here.

I will first examine the hypothesis that a correlation exists between the structural resolutions of themes and volume sales. The χ^2 analysis is used to estimate the goodness of fit between the ECDs and the relevant sales figures. The basic formula used to compute the value of the χ^2 statistic is:

$$\chi^2 = \sum_{i=1}^{r} \sum_{j=1}^{k} \frac{(O_{ij} - E_{ij})^2}{E_{ij}}$$

where: O_{ij} are the observed frequencies, and
E_{ij} are the expected frequencies.
The E_{ij} is computed by the following formula:

$$E_{ij} = \frac{\left(\sum_{m=1}^{k} O_{im}\right)\left(\sum_{n=1}^{r} O_{nj}\right)}{\sum_{n=1}^{r} \sum_{m=1}^{k} O_{nm}}$$

The results should be treated with a degree of caution for reasons which are elaborated below. In order to be able to attach the relevant sales figures to the actual appearance of the commercials, the dates at which the transmissions took place are indispensable. But as each commercial is not transmitted just once but several times one is faced with three possible courses of action.

It can be argued that the first transmission period is the most effective and, therefore, only the sales figures which are relevant to this period should be considered. On the assumption that the frequency of transmission is higher during the first period of a new launch, there is a good reason to expect that the dates for the first transmission period provide one with the relevant information for the most intensive part of the campaign. The first transmission period covers a time span of four weeks.

The second alternative is to take every transmission into account and to assume that each exposure of the commercial is equally effective. The final effect on sales figures is then a compound of the underlying ECD and the number of transmissions for each commercial. As it is assumed that all the transmissions are equally effective, the efficiency of each ECD could be said to be the multiple of the number of transmissions, or some other weighted figure of them. However, it is extremely difficult to separate out, in this case, the effect of the ECD from the effect of the number of transmissions.

The third possibility is to assume that the number of transmissions is important but that they do not all have the same effect, i.e., their efficacy changes with time, viz. number of exposures. If such a stipulation is made it becomes necessary to postulate the way in which the function of efficacy behaves. One such assumption may be that advertising decays geometrically at a constant rate, where the first transmission period is thought to be the most effective and every subsequent transmission period proportionately less effective. The decay coefficient of advertising indicates the rate at which the campaign loses its efficacy, or alternatively the spillover effect of preceding advertising periods on the period examined. In this manner it is theoretically possible to measure for each ECD both the level of efficiency at which it operates and the rate at which this efficiency declines. Though this procedure is both widely used and tempting, for it seems to avoid the pitfalls of the other two, it is felt that there is no real justification for postulating a geometric decline; and the assumption that peak effectiveness is reached in the initial period is subjected to many constraints. The fact that this model is nevertheless used, stems from the ignorance which pervades the whole field of evaluation of advertising efficacy, and the remarkable scarcity of solid data which would make advertising truly accountable. In the absence of any conclusive consensus on the subject it is but reasonable to begin with fairly simple assumptions.

As a digression it may be suggested that a Poisson rather than a geometric distribution may be found to be more satisfactory, for it postulates an initial improvement which reaches its peak after a limited number of transmissions and then proceeds gradually to decline. Unlike the geometric model, the rate of decline is not constant. In this manner two pitfalls are escaped: first, it does not assume that the initial exposure period is necessarily the most effective one, but more realistically that initially efficacy increases with repetition. And second, it does not assume that decay is uniform, thus introducing a greater degree of flexibility into the system of evaluation. However, this approach is very complex and the relevant decay rates are unknown and must be estimated.

As the unknowns of the situation are too many, a complex statistical estimation procedure is unlikely to contribute much to our knowledge. Therefore, I decided to adhere to the first assumption, which while declining to take some factors into account is not constrained by precarious assumptions. At the same time there is a price to be paid in the form of a sharp restriction on the total number of observations. This is equal now to the number of different commercials in the campaign for which market data was available—twenty-nine in all. The statistical reliability of the results is thus somewhat less and one should treat them with a degree of caution.

It is assumed that a 'spillover' effect is characteristic of advertising, and consequently the impact of a campaign can be detected not only throughout the period in which advertising actually takes place but also in subsequent periods. Accordingly, the analysis is pursued in two steps: first an analysis of the period of the campaign itself is undertaken, and then of the period immediately following it.

The null hypothesis H_0 is that there is no relation between the ECD dimensions and volume sales. The contingency table of the observed frequencies in the first period of transmission is shown below.

Observed frequencies

| Exhaustive Common Denominator | Volume sales '000 units | | |
	2300–2900	2901–3500	
Endogenous/exogenous	7	0	7
Eternal time/profane time	2	3	5
Happiness/misery	1	5	6
Knowledge/ignorance	3	2	5
Nature/culture	5	1	6
	18	11	29

The expected frequencies under H_0 are shown in the table below.

Expected frequencies

Exhaustive Common Denominator	Volume sales '000 units		
	2300–2900	2901–3500	
Endogenous/exogenous	4·34	2·66	7
External time/profane time	3·10	1·90	5
Happiness/misery	3·72	2·28	6
Knowledge/ignorance	3·10	1·90	5
Nature/culture	3·72	2·28	6
	18	11	29

$\chi^2 = 11\cdot73$

The critical values for χ^2 at a level of significance, $a = \cdot02$, is $\chi^2\cdot_{98} = 9\cdot49$; therefore, it is possible to reject the null hypothesis, that there is no correlation between the ECDs and volume sales, and accept the alternative hypothesis that such a correlation, subjected to the above qualifications, exists.

One may proceed now to examine the influence of an advertising campaign not at the period at which it is launched but at a subsequent period t_i, which in this context is one month later. The assumption underlying this stipulation is that there is a time-lag between the first launch and actual consumption action, a lag during which subsequent transmissions up to a certain limit fortify the message and allow the campaign to achieve, on the Poisson curve assumption, maximum effectivity. The null hypothesis remains the same and the observed frequencies of period t_i are shown in the following table.

Observed frequencies

Exhaustive Common Denominator	Volume sales '000 units		
	2300–2900	2901–3500	
Endogenous/exogenous	7	0	7
External time/profane time	3	2	5

Happiness/misery	3	3	6
Knowledge/ignorance	0	5	5
Nature/culture	2	4	6
	15	14	29

The expected frequencies under H_0 are shown in the following table.

Expected frequencies

	Volume sales '000 units		
Exhaustive Common Denominator	2300–2900	2901–3500	
Endogenous/exogenous	3·62	3·38	7
External time/profane time	2·59	2·41	5
Happiness/misery	3·10	2·90	6
Knowledge/ignorance	2·59	2·41	5
Nature/culture	3·10	2·90	6
	15	14	29

$\chi^2 = 12·85$

The null hypothesis is rejected yet again at $\chi^2._{98} = 9·49$, and the alternative hypothesis that there is a significant correlation between the variables is accepted.

In order to establish the degree of dependence or association between the measured variables, a reference must be made to the coefficient of contingency, C, which is given by:

$$C = \sqrt{\frac{\chi^2}{\chi^2 + N}}$$

and $0 \leq C \leq 1$

The result for period t_0 is $C = 0·53$ and for period t_1, $C = 0·55$. When $C = 0$ there is no association between the variables and the larger the value of C, the greater is the degree of association. One may conclude then that the degree of association between the variables is satisfactory and that in period t_1 the degree of dependence is slightly higher than in period t_0. Thus the general effectiveness of a campaign is slightly better in the subsequent period than in the period of launch, provided that there is no large time-lag between the two periods.

So far I have tested, using the χ^2 analysis, the goodness of fit between the groups defined by the structural dimensions and volume sales. A significant correlation was found between the variables at ·98 level of confidence. The coefficient of contingency measuring the association between the variables is high and a little stronger for the subsequent period.

Tentative conclusions: ECDs and consumer response

Having concluded that a significant correlation exists between the ECDs and volume sales, a further question may be posed which concerns the direction that this relation takes. It is known from previous analysis that each dimension has a distinct impact on volume sales; the nature of this impact, however, is unknown. In particular, one does not know whether certain structural themes have a positive or a negative effect on the market. Furthermore, it is not clear whether it is possible to assume a uniform impact, positive or negative, of the same dimension across different product areas. In other words, it is not certain whether the dimensions have a power all their own, which is independent of the specific systems of appearances in which they are manifested, or whether the impact they have is dependent on the product area in question so that they could not be dissociated from the particular products advocated. For instance, the theme good : evil $\simeq$ brand X : not brand X, may be extremely effective as far as detergents are concerned; it could also be either very ineffective (or very effective) if the propagated product were something else.

It is impossible, within the limited boundaries of this inquiry, to investigate the consistency of the impact across different product areas, though this is undoubtedly one of the more interesting subjects for further research. At this stage one merely tries to establish, holding all the other dimensions constant, the net effect of each dimension on volume sales. To accomplish this an econometric demand analysis model employing dummy variables (in this case the ECDs) is used.

This model consists of a series of linear equations, where it is assumed that the dependent variable (volume sales) is a function of some independent variables such as price, income, advertising expenditure, and temperature, as well as, one stipulates, of the ECDs. The model is linear. It must be realized, though, that there is no justification for this postulate other than the state of the present knowledge and, of course, convenience. In the darkness in which one is groping, the only sensible assumptions to make must be simple ones. There is no point in stipulating complicated relations when there is no inkling of information on which to base these speculations. From the statistical point of view, a series of linear equations, if fitted in parts, is in many cases a sufficiently close approximation to a function which in itself is non-linear. In this very tentative attempt at measurement, one deliberately opts for the simpler rather than the more complex course of action in the hope of establishing a starting point from which further inquiries could be carried out.

The general equation is:

$$S_t = a + bA + cT + \alpha D_1 + \beta D_2 + \gamma D_3 + \delta D_4 + \theta D_5 + dP_r + u$$

where: S_t —volume sales
$\quad a$ —constant term
$\quad A$ —advertising expenditure
$\quad T$ —temperature
$\quad P_r$ —real prices
$\quad D_{1-5}$—ECD_{1-5}
$\quad u$ —residual
$\quad b, c, d, \alpha, \beta, \gamma, \delta, \theta$ —variable coefficients

The general equation may be broken down into smaller equations each reflecting the net effect of each ECD on volume sales when the other ECDs are held constant. Thus for ECD_1 the equation is:

$$S_{t0} = a + bA + cT + dP_r + \alpha D_{2345 \cdot 01}$$

where $D_{2345 \cdot 01}$ is the impact of ECD_1 on volume sales in period t_0, when all the other ECDs are held constant. The net impact of D_1 is determined by its coefficient, a, and the total advertising impact for dimension one, in the short run, is:

$$b + a$$

and in the long run:

$$\frac{b + a}{1 - \lambda}$$

where λ is the rate of advertising decay.

The same operation is repeated with the other dummies.

Multiple regression analysis consists of curve fitting using the least-squares estimate and it results in a correlation coefficient which indicates what proportion of the variance is explained by the independent variables. It also measures the effect of a marginal change in the independent variables on volume sales and the standard error attached to each one of these variables. The units of measurement are specifically determined for each variable, e.g. in the case of temperature the marginal unit is $1°C$, while in the case of advertising expenditure it is an extra £1000 invested.

In general form, if $y(t)$ is the dependent variable, $x_i(t)$ the independent variable terms, and $w(t)$ a set of weighting factors, the programme chooses a constant c and coefficients a_i so as to minimize the sum of squares:

$$\sum_{t=s}^{p} w(t) \{y(t) - c - \sum i \, a_i \, x_i(t)\}^2$$

where s and p are 'start time' and 'finish time' respectively.

If X is the M by K matrix, $x_i(t)$, (with $x_0(t) = 1$ if the constant is included); and $i = 0, \ldots, K-1$; $t = s, \ldots, P$; then, skipping the vigorous mathematics involved, $X'y$ is the K vector:

$$\sum_{t} w(t) y(t) x_i(t);$$

and the vector of coefficients is then:

$$(a_i) = (X' X)^{-1} X' y$$

The multiple regression coefficient about the mean is:

$$R^2 = 1 + \frac{\sum_t wy - (a_i) \ 'X' y}{\sum_t wy^2 / \sum_t w - \sum_t wy^2}$$

The standard error of (a_i), the regression coefficient of the i'th independent variable, is given by:

$$\sqrt{V(i,j)}$$

where, $V(i,j) = S^2 (X' X)^{-1}$

S^2 is the variance and is defined as:

$$S^2 = \frac{\sum_t wy^2 - (a_i) \ 'X' y}{(M-K)}$$

These are the basic formulae used by the particular computer programme chosen for the multiple regression analysis carried out here.

The number of monthly periods for which information is available is fifty-one. The data used in computing the coefficients are volume sales during these fifty-one periods, advertising expenditure, temperature (which was found to be relevant to this market in a previous investigation) and real prices (which are obtained by deflating money prices by the monthly cost-of-living index). Finally, the ECDs were introduced using the advertising expenditure spent on each dimension as a surrogate. When more than one ECD is used simultaneously with others, the allocation of advertising expenditure to the different dimensions is done in proportion to the number of transmissions of each dimension. The frequency of transmission for each sign is given in the following table.

Dates and frequencies of transmission of the ECDs

Date	Endogenous/ exogenous	Eternal time/ profane time	Happiness/ misery	Knowledge/ ignorance	Nature/ culture
1967					
9	2				
10	2				
11	2				
12	1				
1968					
1	5				
2	1				
3	6				
4	3				
5	3				
6	22				
7	8				
8	1				
9	2				
10	1				
11	1				
12	—				
1969					
1	7	3			
2	1	3	4		
3		6	13		
4		6	9		
5		8	12		
6		7	15		
7		3	2		
8		1	3		
9		8	21		
10		2	7		
11		2	5		
12		—	—		
1970					
1				9	
2				21	
3				18	
4				12	
5				16	
6				19	

Date	Endogenous/exogenous	Eternal time/profane time	Happiness/misery	Knowledge/ignorance	Nature/culture
7				—	
8				1	
9				17	
10				16	
11				11	
12				1	
1971					
1				3	12
2				3	8
3				4	12
4				7	6
5				1	5
6				5	12
7				—	—
8				—	—
9				3	4
10				4	17
11				2	7
12				1	7
Total	68	49	91	174	90

Thus the advertising expenditure, A_t, for June 1971, for instance, is allocated between Knowledge/Ignorance and Nature/Culture in proportion to $5/17$ and $12/17$ correspondingly, and so on for each overlapping period.

The analysis resulted in a correlation coefficient of $R^2 = \cdot48$, which is not particularly strong. However, a few 'mitigating' considerations are in order here. The basis of the data is monthly figures which inevitably tend to register sharper fluctuations than quarterly or yearly figures. As a result the variance is large, and the part which is explainable by the independent variables tends to be more limited. It was impossible to use any other basis because this immediately reduces the number of total observations, which for the purposes of this analysis must not be too small. On a quarterly basis, for instance, I would have only seventeen observations which is not sufficient to establish a clear pattern. The monthly fluctuations are shown in Figure 4.

The experimental nature of this analysis must be emphasized again. I have tried to represent a highly abstract concept in figures that are necessarily approximate. Under these circumstances it might have been rather worrying if the results had been

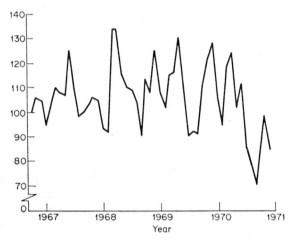

Fig. 4. Volume sales index by monthly periods
(September 1967 = 100).

exceptionally good, for it could have been reasonably suspected that the figures measured something else.

The coefficients of the dummy variables and their standard errors are given in the table below.

Exhaustive Common Denominator	Regression coefficients	Standard error of coefficients
Endogenous/exogenous	−5·56816−01	3·56807+00
Eternal time/profane time	−2·16819+01	1·44504+01
Happiness/misery	1·44919+01	7·95219+00
Knowledge/ignorance	1·67190−01	3·09627−01
Nature/culture	−2·12130+00	4·30719+00

The table should be interpreted in the following manner. For every extra £1000 spent on any of the ECDs there is an increase or a decrease in volume sales (which is measured in '000 units) at the rates indicated by the coefficients above. Thus for every extra £1000 spent on the Endogenous/Exogenous ECD there is a loss of unit sales amounting to 556·8 units, and for every extra £1000 spent on the Happiness/Misery ECD there is an increase in sales amounting to 14 491 units, and so on for the other ECDs.

In order to test the results for significance, the standard error must be taken into account and a region of confidence determined. The confidence interval naturally varies with the level of significance at which one wishes to proclaim the results. In the case of Knowledge/Ignorance, for instance, the distribution may be presented as in the following diagram, where the confidence interval ranges between −618 and +785 with a coefficient of +167 units for every extra £1000 spent.

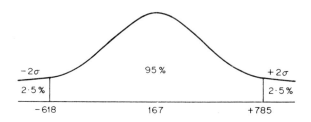

The results are statistically significant at the ·05 level of significance for Happiness/Misery with a statistic of 1·83 > 1·68, and for Eternal Time/Profane Time at $a = ·10$ with a t statistic 1·50 > 1·30. The results are not significant for the other dimensions.

Yet in this instance it is not the statistical significance of the results which are the most immediate concern, but the marketing implications stemming from them. If the unit sales are multiplied by the price, the money value of the impact is obtained. It is then possible, in terms of actual policy formulation, to make up one's mind whether the worst possibility is one which is still acceptable. If the risk involved in taking the worst outcome is still considered to be worth while, then the statistical significance is, for all practical purposes, rather less important.

One may wish to scrutinize the total effect of advertising, expenditure and ECD together, on sales. Only the short-term impact is considered. The advertising expenditure coefficient is

$(7.76466 - 01) \pm (1.11006 + 00)$. The total advertising effects for each one of the structural dimensions are shown in the table below.

Exhaustive Common Denominator	Regression coefficients
Endogenous/exogenous	776 − 556
Eternal time/profane time	776 − 21681
Happiness/misery	776 + 14491
Knowledge/ignorance	776 + 167
Nature/culture	776 − 2121

The total effect of an extra £1000 spent on advertising expenditure for Nature/Culture is $(-1345) \pm (5417)$ for a confidence interval of 67·5 per cent, or $(-1345) \pm (10\ 834)$ for a confidence interval of 95 per cent, and so on for the other dimensions. The marketing interpretation is similar to the one outlined above.

It is clear that in this case, whether one considers the net impact of each ECD or the total impact of advertising expenditure spent on each dimension, the most efficient symbol is Happiness/ Misery and the least efficient, indeed a dimension with a strong negative impact, is Eternal Time/Profane Time. The ECDs rank in accordance with their relative efficacy in the following manner:

1. Happiness/Misery
2. Knowledge/Ignorance
3. Endogenous/Exogenous
4. Nature/Culture
5. Eternal Time/Profane Time

Some dimensions appear concurrently, yet it is possible to separate the net effect of each. Knowledge/Ignorance and Nature/Culture are transmitted alternately during the same periods, yet while the first is relatively efficient, the latter is relatively inefficient. It is reasonable to assume that the combination of the two is likely to undermine the efficacy of the efficient as a result of the confusion caused in the perception of the underlying themes, and that the net result of any campaign is always a reflection of the precarious balance achieved by confused and, therefore, confusing messages.

Finally, an attempt has been made to introduce the geometric decay variable into the original demand analysis, to examine whether the original correlation might not be stronger, as a result of this correcting factor. The decay coefficient reflects the rate at which the effect of previous advertising declines and the general decrease in the effectivity of the campaign. The correlation coefficient is now slightly improved at $R^2 = \cdot 53$, and the decay rate is $\lambda = \cdot 26$ in the short term and $\lambda = \dfrac{b}{1 - \cdot 26}$ in the long term. It might be remembered that b is the coefficient of advertising expenditure. Summarizing the main conclusions of the analysis, the limited statistical investigation carried out so far seems to suggest two main conclusions:

(a) At the $\cdot 98$ confidence interval a significant correlation was found to exist between the ECD dimensions and consumer response as measured by volume sales. This correlation is valid both during the campaign and during the period immediately following the campaign. The correlation for any subsequent periods was not tested.

(b) It is possible tentatively to conclude that the dimensions have different impacts on consumer's response, some affecting it positively and others negatively. The most effective campaign, according to the present analysis, is the one using Happiness/Misery, and the least effective is Eternal Time/Profane Time.

The analysis has been delimited to some of the more obvious and narrow aspects of the problem. The two questions posed and the answers to them are but first steps towards a better understanding.

A number of questions have remained unanswered. First, one is completely ignorant of the interaction effect of 'joint' campaigns which are carried out simultaneously. It is unknown whether this detracts from the force of the more effective campaign (though it is plausible to assume so), or whether it makes it more effective as a result of this forced juxtaposition. One may hypothesize, though, that simultaneous campaigns employing different dimensions contribute to a 'jamming' effect in the network and thus increase the degree of noise in the system.

Second, one does not know whether the underlying themes have a uniform effect in all systems of propagation, or whether the impact, as identified above, pertains to the product under consideration only. To be able to throw light on this question, better techniques must be utilized and the analysis should be carried out on a large number of products.

Third, it is plausible to assume that, apart from the individual effect of each sign, there could also be a system effect, which is not simply additive but a tangible something quite above and beyond the combined effect of the ECDs.

Fourth, it is reasonable to assume, and this is in a sense an extension of the first point, that there is a spillover effect from previous campaigns controlled by one ECD on to the campaigns under consideration, so that the so-called net effect of any current campaign reflects also a residual value, which could be either positive or negative, of previous campaigns. One leaves this area with more problems unsolved than solved, yet it is felt that the results on the whole are sufficiently encouraging to merit further research. However, this is beyond the scope of this work.

References

In the statistical and econometric analysis the following books and publications were used:

1. J. J. Johnston, *Econometric Methods* (McGraw-Hill, 1963).
2. M. R. Spiegel, *Theory and Problems of Statistics* (New York: Schaum Publishing Co., 1961).
3. S. Siegel, *Nonparametric Statistics for the Behavioural Sciences* (McGraw-Hill, 1956).
4. T. H. Wonnacott and R. J. Wonnacott, *Introductory Statistics* (John Wiley, 1969).
5. J. A. C. Brown, 'On the use of covariance techniques in demand analysis', mimeographed (Cambridge: Department of Applied Economics, University of Cambridge, 1958). Available on request.

6. Structure and function

Que la réalité vraie n'est jamais la plus manifeste; et que la nature du vrai transparaît déjà dans le soin qu'il met à se dérober. Lévi-Strauss

The time has come to string together all the hints I have dropped so far into a coherent general statement. One may begin by placing the advertising campaigns I have hitherto discussed on a schematic map, showing which levels of advertising and what types of campaign have been considered in Chapters 3 and 4.

All along an implicit distinction has been drawn between a product and a brand. This distinction simply implies that any product idea may be realized in different packages, with different names and different advertising—in short, in a distinct general presentation. A product could have many forms, and the forms are but the clothes which conceal the product. A product without a brand is a commodity, and the brand is the cloak enfolding the commodity. Naturally, these remarks are restricted to the type of products I have chosen to analyse.

The advertising game is most common between the perfectly substitutable manifestations of the same product. It is precisely one of the tasks of advertising to expose this substitutability as unwarranted by creating unique images—identities which cannot be crushed. Advertising is further used in the war between substitutable products, such as tea and coffee, butter and margarine, and so on. From one point of view such campaigns are but a private case of the previous one, for the basic intention to persuade the consumer to switch from one thing to another, or to remain a firm believer in the product he already consumes, is unaltered. The consumer, however, perceives the struggle for prominence between two products as vastly different from the one between brands. These battles are fought on different

119

grounds, for different causes, using different ammunition. Finally, there are two relatively infrequent cases in which advertising is devoted to the advocacy of a single brand or a single product. In both cases, competition in itself is rather less important. The reasons for the campaign are to introduce a new product and provide information about it, as well as, and this is perhaps the most important aspect of this type of advertising, to maintain its prominence with and provide reinforcement to its present users. It may be remembered that advertising is not merely concerned with attracting usership from one product/brand to another—a state of affairs which is bound to result in some sort of a precarious balance as all the competitors are engaged in an activity which is essentially the same—but also with the fortification of an already acquired habit. The campaigns I have examined so far are depicted in the diagram overleaf.

Great English Cheese against New Zealand Cheese, and Washing Powder A against Washing Powder B are intra-group campaigns. Baby Foods and Margarine are comprehensive product group campaigns. Margarine against Butter, on the other hand, are inter-group competitive campaigns while Brand E and Cheese are dominant brand campaigns. The overlap between Brand R and the product area to which it belongs is such that it is permitted to consider Brand R as being virtually equal to the product area. The advertising advocating Brand R is an intra-group universal campaign. The nine major representations examined so far cover, therefore, all the basic targets of advertising.

There is, however, one exception, in which the anomaly consists of a strange contest between brands which are neither competitive nor substitutable, and which nevertheless enter into binary relations with each other. I refer to spreading against baking where the distinction, in a rather odd manner, pertains to the differentiation of function rather than of identity. One could argue quite convincingly that baking margarine and spreading margarine are not different brands belonging to the same product area, but simply different products which happen to have a common name. Yet naming is an act of classification, and even though the products differ in function, texture, colour and general presentation, they still belong together because they are all margarine. Category building in the consumer's mind persists in

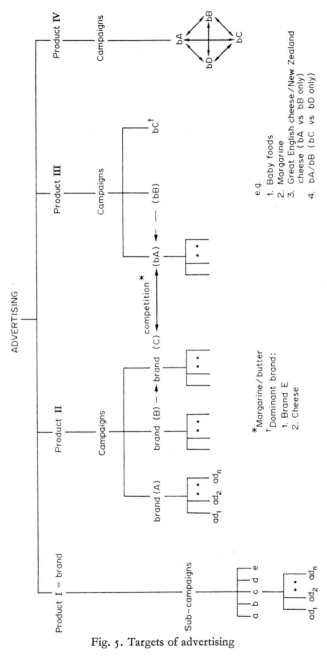

Fig. 5. Targets of advertising

spite of the obvious logical and practical advantages of other classifications. One such possibility is to consider butter and spreading margarine as one product, which is realized in different brands of distinguishable flavours and textures. The possible combinations are, therefore, not two but four:

butter/margarine   —competitive, substitutable
                     (overall inter-product competition)
baking/baking   —competitive, substitutable
spreading/spreading—competitive, substitutable
baking/spreading   —non-competitive, non-substitutable

Of these four possibilities I have explored the first and fourth.

Having placed the campaigns in their proper perspective, one may turn now to the main discussion. Advertising is conceived of as a process of mediation par excellence. So far, three inter-related manifestations of the mediating character of advertising have been discussed. First, and this is strictly limited to the surface manifestations, advertising is conceived of as an inter-mediary mechanism between social values and consumption behaviour. As such, it includes what Leibenstein admirably defined as 'bandwagon', 'snob' and 'Veblen' effects.[1] The 'bandwagon effect' is 'the desire of people to wear, buy, do, consume, and behave like their fellows; the desire to join the crowd, be "one of the boys", etc.—phenomena of mob motiva-tion and mass psychology either in their grosser or more delicate aspects.'[2] It is 'the extent to which the demand for a commodity is *increased* due to the fact that others are also consuming the same commodity.'[3] The 'snob effect' refers to the 'extent to which demand for a consumers' good is *decreased* owing to the fact that others are also consuming the same commodity. This represents the desire of people to be exclusive, to be different; to dissociate themselves from the "common herd".'[4] By 'Veblen effect', Leibenstein refers to 'the phenomenon of conspicuous con-sumption; to the extent to which the demand for a consumers' good is increased because it bears a higher rather than lower price.'[5] While the snob effect is a function of the consumption of others, the Veblen effect is a function of price. However, both motivations derive from a desire for prestige.

Rephrasing the above definitions in sociological terminology, the bandwagon effect is mostly concerned with the desire for social acceptability. This is accomplished through conformity to the prevailing system of values, through a strict adherence to the code of conduct characteristic of the reference group of one's choice. Snob and Veblen effects emphasize, on the other hand, the values of individuality, success and exclusivity. While the bandwagon effect reflects the desire to be like the generalized other, the snob-Veblen effects reflect the desire to be an exalted looking-glass self.

All these values are, either explicitly or implicitly, encouraged by affluent societies. Indeed some are fundamental to the existence of these societies in their present form. Notwithstanding this fact, advertising enjoys special notoriety which lends itself open to attacks not only by the opposers of the system but also by its supporters. For the opposers the cardinal sin of advertising is in being a pillar of modern mass-consumption mass-production economy. As such it helps to perpetuate the existing social and economic order. It is no less than a modern Mephistopheles. It tempts the consumer to buy superfluous things and creates unnecessary wants. It makes people compete destructively and channels their energy in wrong directions. It exploits human frailty in the interests of commerce. And its methods are manipulative and exploitative.

Moreover, the rejection of advertising is not merely a reflection of a criticism fraught with foreboding of a society destined to a lifeless, materialistic doom, but more particularly an expression of a deep fear for the safety of a second pillar of modern life, that of rationality. The ascetic observer of the Protestant ethic, not only wishes to protect an honourable way of life, which is devoid of frivolity and devoted to hard work and simple living, but also to fortify the inner walls of consciousness against the invasion of archaic irrationality.[6] I will return to this problem in the next chapter.

In my terminology the surface manifestation mediates much of what McLuhan considers to be the subliminal or the unconscious appeal of advertising.[7] I do not believe that either the suggestibility of advertising or the chain of associations created by clever juxtapositions properly belongs in the area of the unconscious. It is felt that advertising, like language, is constrained by certain deep structures which are alone reflected, as if in a set of twisted mirrors, in the advertising system of appearances. McLuhan's unconscious is semi-conscious, for his advertiser, like a true artist, is perfectly aware of what he is accomplishing.

I have maintained so far that advertising is, on the surface level, a process of mediation between social values and consumption behaviour, and on the deep level an intermediary mechanism between fundamental cultural themes and consumer preferences. Advertising, however, has a 'second' existence which is quite separate and independent of other external systems and which is devoted, in the seclusion of its own vitality, to the processing of images and to the perpetual game of concretization and abstraction. Advertising is regarded as a closed system of appearances. Every mental representation in it inevitably ascends and descends the ladder erected between the two poles: the abstract and the concrete. It is thus, that the second role of advertising, as an intermediary mechanism, concerns the mediation of the abstract into the concrete and vice versa. How this is accomplished was described in chapters 3 and 4.

Third, advertising is the process of mediation between the consumer and the producer. As such it is predominantly concerned with the communication of goods and services and with the creation, expansion and maintenance of consumer markets. It is the mental avenue through which the images of goods are processed on the way to their final destination. Advertising uses the discourse of images to bring about the dialogue of values.

These observations are straightforward enough; yet is it not possible that, having constructed these models which strive to explain the nature of advertising, one has simultaneously erected a screen which makes the real view opaque? For it now seems that advertising is all it has been claimed to be so far, and more. The previous observations suggest very strongly that advertising is the prototype, indeed the locus of all communication.

Lévi-Strauss observes that societies have only three types of communications, or indeed only one process of communication which is manifested on three different levels; those of messages, women and goods.[8] Though all three are forms of communication they do not operate on the same scale:

> Thus, from marriage to language one passes from low to high-speed communication; this arises from the fact that what is

communicated in marriage is almost of the same nature as those who communicate (women, on the one hand, men, on the other), while speakers of language are not of the same nature as their utterances. The opposition is thus one of *person* to *symbol*, or of *value* to *sign*. This helps to clarify the somewhat intermediate position of economics between these two extremes—goods and services are not persons, but they still are values. And, though neither symbols nor signs, they require symbols or signs in order to be successfully exchanged when the exchange system reaches a certain degree of complexity.[9]

Thus, advertising is the complex of images, symbols, signs and messages which is utilized to create the real exchange of goods and services for yet another value, money. Advertising is the sign which allows a value to be exchanged. Exchange of women, in the sense in which Lévi-Strauss uses the term, meets in modern society with minimal constraints, nevertheless it is still a type of communication. Advertising communication is restricted to two levels only, that of message and that of value, in both of which it possesses a singular position. It encompasses in one medium the concern for both, and while using one type of communication, it really applies itself to an exchange which takes place elsewhere. It is a system of signs which devotes itself entirely and exclusively to the exchange of values. Women come into the advertising circle because they are the main target of appeal, at least as far as the type of products analysed here is concerned. Advertising is, in this manner, at the very centre of the process of communication and could justifiably be regarded as the locus of the main communication systems or the communication system par excellence. There are, of course, other exchange systems, which stretch beyond the region of this study, and which involve the transfer of power, money and prestige in areas other than consumption.

The process of advertising is, in this manner, an excellent example of what Shannon defines as levels B and C of communication problems. Level B is the semantic problem, which is concerned with 'the identity, or satisfactory close approximation, in the interpretation of meaning by the receiver, as compared with the intended meaning of the sender.'[10] Level C is the effectiveness problem and concerns 'the success with which the meaning conveyed to the receiver leads to the desired conduct on his part.'[11] It is clear from these definitions that levels B and C together define the successful communication of signs, in the sense that it leads to the type of behaviour urged by the commercial. Levels B and C are in a nutshell what advertising is all about.

It might be remembered that Jacques Durand and Roland Barthes consider advertising to be a manifestation of the art of rhetoric in one of its most accomplished and rich forms. '*On s'aperçoit alors que, si la publicité a un intérêt culturel, c'est à la pureté et à la richesse de sa structure rhétorique qu'elle le doit: non pas à ce qu'elle peut apporter d'information vraie, mais à sa part de fiction.*'[12] It has been further observed that advertising is the art of condensation, for in an incredibly short span of time (or in a skilful use of space) it conveys a message of great complexity, and draws upon a number of intricate systems of expression.

Advertising has so far been defined as the art of rhetoric and condensation, as a mediating process from the abstract to the concrete and finally, and this is a description which encompasses the rest, as a centre of communication processes. I will pursue these leads in the next chapter, and turn meanwhile to other considerations.

It has been suggested in the previous chapters that advertising is a grand system of appearances, which may be broken down into sub-systems organized around *product* representations. Furthermore, these sub-systems can be decoded to reveal their fundamental themes which are called, in the terminology introduced here, the Exhaustive Common Denominators. These dimensions operate at the back of the system of appearances on a level which is, as it were, behind and beneath the surface, and which nevertheless, through many repetitions, is communicated to the spectator in a manner of which neither he nor the advertiser know anything. The level of operation is truly unconscious. Yet the structure of advertising is but an homologous reflection of the way in which the mind works. Advertising, like language or any other system of communication, must abide by certain rules of competence.

Advertisements fight a war on two levels. On the surface level they have to compete with other images, or as McLuhan rather whimsically puts it: 'Real news is *bad* news . . . Ads, in contrast, have to shrill their happy message loud and clear in order to match the penetrating power of bad news.'[13] And on the structural level, in order to convey their deep message, they have first to overcome interference and noise in a system which is particularly badly jammed, and then to surmount the conscious models of interpretation which lure the mind by offering tempting solutions. In order to ensure that the message will push its way through the perceptual barriers, the amount of redundancy displayed is unusually high, and the use of rhetoric becomes necessary for the same reason. On the structural level, the relationship between the constituent parts of a single advertisement and the other members of the system is like the relationship between a single piece in a jigsaw puzzle and the rest of the pieces belonging to the same pattern. Each piece in an ordinary jigsaw puzzle is meaningless till it is brought into a relationship with the other pieces. The case of advertising is more complex because there are in fact two levels of meaning, not one. Each individual advertisement has a meaning in itself in the sense that it tells something about a product or a service. This is the surface meaning. Simultaneously, the constituent parts of each advertisement are elements belonging to a wider system. And so the surface meaning of individual advertisements can change quite dramatically when their constituent parts form the correct and exhaustive relationships with the other constituent parts of the other advertisements belonging to the same system. It is as if each advertisement provides some aspects of the system and together they form the whole system. In this second sense only, individual advertisements are meaningless till they are put into a system of relationships with each other, from which the individual significance of each may emerge.

On the basis of the analysis carried out so far, it is felt that one could maintain with a certain amount of conviction that beyond the obvious manifestation lies another, which though opaque is nevertheless no less real. It is possible, moreover, to reduce all advertising phenomena into a binary structure, which is at once exhaustive and complete. The ECD, as indicated before, is simply a double sign, where the left-most element on the left-hand side is the signifier of the left-most element on the right-hand side (which is the signified); and the right-most element on the left-hand side is the signifier of the signified, which is the right-most element on the right-hand side ($a : b \simeq c : d$ where a signifies c and b signifies d). One may proceed, now, to discuss some special problems.

The analysis was very conveniently divided into two demon-strations, one devoted to static advertising and the other to dynamic advertising. The general differences between the two media are discussed in Chapter 4. However, there is one point which has been reserved till now. This does not concern the media directly, but the constraints that it imposes on the 'storage' of a sample.

It is possible to collect all the magazine advertisements which appear during a certain period of time and which pertain to particular goods. It inevitably means that the sample consists of a fairly large number of advertisements which represent a number of brands in their proper product areas. In terms of Figure 5, the analysis in most cases is done on a multi-brand basis. In my case, for instance, having selected the sample in this manner, I subjected the system of appearances to a process of deciphering, with the special object in mind of testing the initial hypothesis, namely that underlying the system of appearances is a structure, and that it is possible to demonstrate that such a structure exists. Dynamic images, on the other hand, are particularly difficult to record and to store without sophisticated equipment, such as a video tape-recorder and monitor. It was for this reason (which prevented me from recording commercials as they were trans-mitted), and because I assumed (wrongly) that brand campaigns form lawful sub-systems within the general advertising system, that the decision fell on a number of campaigns for specific brands.

To reiterate, the main difference between static advertising and dynamic advertising, in terms of the sample of advertisements, is that in the first instance the advertisements mostly form the system of appearances of product areas. In the second instance, however, the sample was severely restricted to the images of one brand at a time. This disparity, of which initially I thought nothing, turned out to be a distinction of major importance. A journey into the unknown is bound to result in some trial and error.

It may be remembered that I started with six general brand campaigns, each covering a period of four years. Of these six general campaigns, which were initially considered to be legiti-mate systems, only two were decipherable. The other four resisted all attacks and stubbornly refused to obey any kind of systematic arrangement; more specifically, the constituent units did not enter into binary relations with each other. Thus, these four general campaigns have not passed even the first test which demands that all the elementary segments of a campaign must be arranged in binary oppositions, let alone the second much more stringent test, that of reducing the two sides of the equations into one Exhaustive Common Denominator. Given the circumstances I had two alternatives: either to abandon the theory on the ground that it failed to achieve its purposes, or to search for a flaw in the reasoning or procedure. Needless to say the second course was taken, not because of any strong allegiance to a theory I merely tried to test at the time, but because of two important considerations, which emerged from the preceding analysis.

The first consideration concerns the very odd difference between static and dynamic advertising. In the former, the difficulty of deciphering the code was relatively small, while in the latter it was, in fact, impossible to decipher it. The second interesting factor to emerge is that in the sample of six dynamic general campaigns, two yielded their secrets quite willingly, while the others remained mute.

Now, there is no inherent reason at all, why static advertising should be more readily susceptible to structural analysis than dynamic advertising. And the second puzzle is why certain types of brand campaigns should be decipherable, while others are indecipherable. Putting these two factors together, one realizes that the fundamental difference between the decodable and the undecodable concerns the characteristics of the sample. In other words, and more sharply defined, the basic differentiating aspect impinges upon the implicit definition of what constitutes a lawful system. While in static advertising this was defined to be all the representations relating to a *product* area, in dynamic advertising this was defined as all the images pertaining to a *brand*. It might be remembered that a structure can be identified only in a system, and not in aggregates or unrelated members of a system. As Piaget warns: 'the laws governing a structure's composition are not reducible to cumulative one-by-one associations of its elements: they confer on the whole as such over-all properties distinct from the properties of its elements.'[14]

At this point the simple and, perhaps, the most logical explanation of the puzzle presents itself. The error I made was to assume that it is possible to break the advertising system into legitimate sub-sub-systems, i.e., to regard brand appearances as an admissible sub-system.* This is patently wrong. Let me clarify the terminology first. As was shown earlier there are only three types of advertising: (*a*) advertising of a number of competitive brands† in the same product field. This is the case of the perfectly substitutible brands, for instance, TV sets, washing powders, sweets, package tours, etc. (*b*) The second category involves advertising of competing substitutes which are not identical, e.g. butter and margarine; tea and coffee. The war can be either between product groups *in toto* (e.g. cheese against meat), as specific brands in each group fight against specific brands of the other group (e.g. Nestle coffee against Brooke Bond Tea), or indeed one brand fighting the other product area at large (e.g. New Zealand cheddar against meat). (*c*) The third and final possibility is the advertising of a single brand. When this brand is unique it is in fact the whole product field. Another type enjoying a similar position is the dominant brand which has a high share of the market of the particular product.

With one exception, the minimum system level is the system of appearances of a *product* or, in other words, all the representations of brands making up the product system. So, all the commercials for all the advertised toothpastes will form one legitimate system; but all the commercials for Colgate alone will never form an admissible system. The images of a single competitive brand alone never form a system. Consequently, it is impossible to exhaust a system if only certain fragments of the whole are considered. While this conclusion may seem obvious, it impinges upon one of the most difficult problems in structuralism, which is the definition of a system. It is not always easy to tell in advance what the frontiers of a system are, and which breakdowns of one system into sub-systems are viable, in the sense that they

* If advertising at large for all products and all services is regarded as the grand system of advertising, then the system of appearances of one *product* area is a sub-system of this grand system. The representations of each brand within the advertising system of a product form the sub-sub-system of the grand system of advertising.

† A competitive brand is defined as one brand among a number of brands none of which dominates the market, and all of which belong to the same product area.

are reducible to a structure. Thus the conclusion that all the representations of a competitive brand never constitute a system is far reaching and by no means apparent. The only circumstance in which the appearances of a brand form a genuine system is, when the brand either equals the product, i.e., the product area consists of one brand only, or when it happens to be a very dominant brand which is faced with little competition from other brands in the same product area.

Reality, however, is never free from complications. For in the special case of the unique brand, which is by definition equal to a product, a further breakdown into structurally defined sub-systems is possible. The same observation applies in the very similar case of dominant brands. Of course, as is shown in Chapter 4, in the cases of brand E and brand R, these sub-systems are linked together to form one whole. But they do, nevertheless, have an independent existence in the sense that each is reducible and definable by its own double sign. Thus, while tales of *a* brand among brands are a non-system, the individual sub-campaigns of a unique or a dominant brand do form true systems.

The reason why a complete competitive brand campaign does not form a system, and the campaigns of a unique brand do form a system is simple. A competitive brand which is analysed in isolation is unable to form a system, because it is but a series of unrelated fragments, which though belonging to one large jigsaw puzzle, are unable to fall into a coherent pattern so long as the other pieces are missing. It is like a word which is unable to become a part of a sentence so long as other words are not added to it, and so long as the whole group is not linked together in a proper syntactic order. The appearances of a competitive brand provide only bits and pieces of a pattern which is much larger. Alone, and this is in perfect harmony with structuralist theory, it has the potential of becoming a meaningful part of a system, yet in the absence of the whole, it is in itself meaningless; it is like 'the word within the word unable to speak a word.'[15] The unique brand, on the other hand, is a complete product system, which is composed of only one (or one dominant) brand. It is not very surprising that it is susceptible to the process of decoding, as is any other correctly defined system. The reason why even the sub-campaigns of this unique brand are also structurally defined and, consequently, form genuine wholes is related to the function of the structure in communicating the final message. Before explaining what is meant by this statement, I must first discuss another point, the understanding of which is crucial to the present issue.

The previous discussion of what constitutes a lawful system has a very important corollary. The advertising game is played on more than one level of cognition and non-cognition. Advertisers study their own and their competitors' advertisements, striving to identify a claim or a benefit which is more powerful, a treatment which is more effective, and a form which is more striking. Little do they realize that on all levels their creative activity is most strictly constrained by the fundamental rules of the game. In cases of dominant and unique brands as distinct from multi-brand campaigns, in order to make the announcement meaningful to themselves and to their customers, they somehow 'put in' a complete structural definition. In cases of competitive brands, on the other hand, the rules of the game change and each individual brand campaign supplies certain fragmentary pieces which, together with others (and a certain degree of redundancy), form one integral system. Each image is superimposed or juxtaposed upon other images, and all the images together decode the pattern in the puzzle. Unknowingly, the advertiser 'builds in' a complete structure into the various representations of a dominant or a unique brand; while in the case of competitive brands, different advertisers not only advocate the benefits of their special brands, but unconsciously participate in an interaction which is much more profound, and which concerns the construction of the underlying structure. A unique brand, in order to convey a message, must be founded on a structure. This structure is 'built' into its system of appearances by its sole advertiser. The same applies to the joint system of appearances of competitive brands, only there the structure is a result of an unconscious collective effort by different advertisers and the system involves a number of different brands. This cannot be emphasized enough. The existence of a structure is essential to the understanding of the message. Were it not for the structural resolution, the advertisements would remain ambiguous. Their meaning will elude the consumer as well as the advertiser. For a campaign to be meaningful it must have a structure. This is the fundamental reason why the representations of dominant brands form a system, and those of a single competitive brand do not. It solves, within the framework of the structuralist theory, the phenomenon of the non-decipherability of individual competitive brands.

I am now in a position to answer the previous question, which is why the sub-campaigns of a dominant brand are structurally defined. It may be remembered that the campaigns have covered a period of four years, and that for a campaign to become meaningful it must have a structure. As it is impossible to wait for a very long period of time in order to achieve marketing results, it follows that the message of advertising must be put across as speedily and as vigorously as possible. If advertising is unintelligible unless it has a complete structure, then a short period of transmission using a limited number of advertisements must be able to produce a complete structural definition. It is for this reason that unique brand campaigns can, indeed, must be broken down into shorter sub-campaigns, each comprising of a limited number of ads and each being a viable system in its own right. Because a unique brand has no direct competitors it must generate a complete structure on its own. Competitive brands, on the other hand, produce the structure collectively through a process of interaction in the product field. The sub-campaigns of a number of competitive brands will have a structure, while the complete universal campaign for one competitive brand does not.

In order to test this explanatory hypothesis for the initial failure to decode individual competitive campaigns, one needs only to analyse other members of the product field and see whether the joint analysis results in a structural definition. I have attempted to do this by analysing one of the previously indecipherable competitive campaigns against a set of new commercials of another brand in the same product area. Unfortunately, it was impossible to obtain the group of images which describe the other brands in the area.

The analysis in Chapter 4 of brand A and brand B, the case in point, resulted, subject to the reservations discussed there, in a resolution of theme. Not wishing to repeat what was already discussed at length there, only the main conclusion is discussed. Two competing brands do not enter into binary relations, because the comparison between them is drawn on analogous comparative lines, and not in absolute terms. The Exhaustive Common Denominator determines the over-all model of the whole product area. The specific value of each member within this general battlefield is determined by the structural proximity it displays to the fundamental structure of the whole system. The smaller the distance, the more effective it is likely to be. In campaigns for unique products on the other hand, the over-all structural resolution is less important, and it is for this reason that a certain level of experimentation with fundamental themes is present. The over-all model is not yet determined. Messages are tested by a process of trial and error, which is very similar in kind to the one carried out with surface messages, in pursuit of the one which is most effective.

While it may be plausible to assume that some product areas naturally lend themselves to the control of a certain type of basic theme, the state of knowledge at the moment only permits speculation. One would tend to feel that this might be the case, but it is not claimed that the fundamental relations identified in each case are these absolute models. They could merely be steps on the road to the final 'discovery' of the one dimension which is most effective. It is suspected that such an identification has, perhaps, been made in two cases only: washing powders (good/evil), and baby foods (life/death). It may be concluded that the structural resolutions do not always reflect the best solutions and that even in this respect, as is openly admitted for surface messages, experimentation is essential.

One may, finally, touch upon the question of efficacy. It has been shown in the preceding chapter that a significant correlation exists between ECDs and volume sales, and that it is possible to delineate the general direction, positive or negative, in which each ECD affects consumption. The methods employed are regarded as tentative measures of a relation which is, in fact, infinitely more complex. Here, however, one is interested in another aspect of efficacy, which concerns the significance of the underlying structure for the perception of advertising.

Chomsky suggests that the function of the deep structure, as it is defined by him, is to endow a group of sounds with meaning: 'The grammatical functions of the deep structure play a central role in determining the meaning of a sentence.'[16] John Lyons in his discussion of Chomsky's theories succinctly summarizes the fundamentals of transformational grammar, thus:

> The base rules generate an infinitely large set of underlying phrase markers (which represent the *deep structure* of all sentences characterised by the system); and these are converted into derived phrase markers (which represent the *surface structure* of the sentences) by the transformational rules, most of which (apart from 'stylistic' rules) are now obligatory. The meaning of each sentence is derived, mainly if not wholly, from its deep structure, by means of the rules of semantic interpretation; and the phonetic interpetation of each sentence—its physical description as an acoustic 'signal'—is derived from its surface structure by means of the phonological rules.[17]

The ear receives meaningless sounds as the eye takes note of meaningless images. It is only when these signals are processed and interpreted by the mind that they are endowed with meaning.

The so-called ambiguous sentences testify to the existence of deep structures. How does one know that a sentence has more than one sense? The surface arrangement is just the same, the signs received are identical, and yet the meaning could be very different. It is Chomsky's thesis, that while the surface structure is identical in all interpretations, the deep structure is not. The diverse meanings of ambiguous sentences are realized when the proper and different deep structures are evoked.

Confining myself to the problem at hand, I would suggest that advertising is a multi-layers construct, each of which may have its own level of meaning. While the surface level is devoted to product characterization and consumer benefits, and the intermediary level to semi-conscious messages, the underlying dimensions of an advertising system are exhaustive statements, which reduce all the diverse appearances into simultaneously abstract and simple binary relation. It is suggested that having viewed a large number of advertisements relating to a certain product area, the impact which is made on the consumer's mind is the summary and fundamental theme, which he recognizes as the basic message. I cannot quite argue with Chomsky that it is the underlying structure, in the sense that this term is used here, that gives meaning to the surface representations; because the surface structure of advertising possesses a meaning or meanings which are themselves determined by Chomsky's deep structures, in the sense in which he uses the term. In advertising the structure does not determine the meaning of the surface, it is the meaning.

The efficacy of advertising depends (at least in part) on the ability of the advertisement to communicate the deep message to the consumer. In other words, the clarity, simplicity and precision with which the message is coded, or more particularly the degree to which the structure has a high or a low definition, are pertinent to the impact that the campaign may eventually make on the consumer's mind. The more complex the code is, the less efficient the advertisements tend to be, and the more highly defined the structure is, the more effective the campaign is.

The level of definition could be described, in the simplest case, as the number of advertisements one needs to analyse in order to obtain the underlying structure. The smaller this number is, the higher the definition, and vice versa. Thus, if the total number of advertisements is n, and K_{min} is the minimum number of advertisements from which the ECD can be identified, and where $K_{min} \leqq n$, then the level of definition is given as:

$$\xi = \frac{n - K_{min}}{n} = 1 - \frac{K_{min}}{n}$$

One is now in a position to define the two extreme possibilities, of high definition and low definition, using this basic formula.

high definition: when $K_{min} = 1$, then $\xi = 1 - \dfrac{1}{n}$

and, low definition: when $K_{min} = n$, then $\xi = 0$

It is possible to describe the level of definition only when the analysis has been completed, because it is only then that one realizes how many appearances are required in order to identify the ECD. It will be realized too that once the ECD has been identified, its recurrence in additional appearances is strictly speaking redundant. However, from the point of view of perception and recognition, it plays a vital role in hammering in, fortifying and barricading of the initial message.

In practical terms, this has interesting implications. If one assumes, for instance, that the ECD may be identified from the appearance of one advertisement, and then again be identified from the joint representations of three further advertisements, it is possible to argue that the degree of redundancy and repetition necessary for perception, could be produced by repeating the single advertisement, say, three times rather than producing three different advertisements and transmitting them at least nine times.

I have offered in this chapter a theoretical interpretation which delineates some of the main concrete implications of the structuralist approach for advertising. The main conclusions concern the nature of advertising as a process of communication, the criteria of a viable system of appearances with special reference to dominant brands and competitive brands, as well as the implications of structure for the conveyance of meaning and advertising efficacy.

References

1. H. Leibenstein, 'Bandwagon, snob, and Veblen effects in the theory of consumers' demand', *Quarterly Journal of Economics*, vol. 64 (1950), pp. 183–207.
2. Ibid., p. 184.
3. Ibid., p. 189.
4. Ibid.
5. Ibid.
6. D. G. MacRae, 'Advertising and Sociology' in *Ideology and Society* (Heinemann, 1961), pp. 77–86; The Labour Party, *Report of a Commission of Enquiry into Advertising*, Chs V and VI, pp. 128–84.
7. See, for instance, J. Miller, *McLuhan* (Fontana, 1971), pp. 73–5; M. McLuhan, *The Mechanical Bride* (Routledge & Kegan Paul, 1951); McLuhan, *Understanding Media* (McGraw-Hill, 1964), pp. 226–33.
8. C. Lévi-Strauss, *Structural Anthropology* (Allen Lane, 1968), p. 296.
9. Ibid., pp. 296–7.
10. C. E. Shannon and W. Weaver, *The Mathematical Theory of Communication* (Urbana: The University of Illinois Press, 1969), p. 4.
11. Ibid., p. 5.
12. J. Durand, 'Rhétorique et image publicitaire', *Communications*, no. 15 (1970), p. 70.
13. Quoted in S. Finkelstein, *Sense and Nonsense in McLuhan* (New York: International Publishers, 1968), p. 57.
14. J. Piaget, *Structuralism* (Routledge & Kegan Paul, 1971), p. 7.
15. M. McLuhan, *From Cliché to Archetype* (New York: Pocket Books, 1970), p. 109.
16. N. Chomsky, *Language and Mind* (New York: Harcourt, Brace & World, 1968), p. 26.
17. J. Lyons, *Chomsky* (Fontana, 1970), p. 80.

7. The advertising system

'Now for the evidence,' said the king, 'and then the sentence.'
'No!' said the queen, 'first the sentence and then the evidence!'
'Nonsense!' cried Alice, so loudly that everybody jumped, 'the
idea of having the sentence first!'   Lewis Carroll

The previous chapter has dwelt upon the more direct implications of the structure underlying the *activité publicitaire*. Some of the more apparent derivatives of advertising as a symbolic system were discussed without, however, pressing the line of argument to its final logical conclusion. That task is left to this last chapter.

Let us go back to Chapters 3 and 4, where two samples, one composed of static advertisements and the other of dynamic ones, were analysed. It will be remembered that in order to uncover the structure of advertising campaigns a certain process of decoding must be followed. The basic property of this transformation process consists of successive reductions whereby the constituent units are arranged in binary relations, and it culminates in the final reduction to the Exhaustive Common Denominator. It will also be remembered that the process of exhaustion, though enabling one to reduce the system of appearances to its defining principle, does not impoverish the system or detract from its richness. Also, in principle, it is always possible to transform back from the ECD, through the binary formulae, to the initial constituent elements, though the exact rules enabling one to do so have not been specified in this work.

The ECD is not simply a synonymous expression with the binary formulae from which it is derived, in the same way that the binary formulae themselves are not synonymous with each other. Rather, the relations are metaphorical. They are different manifestations on various levels of reality of certain fundamental relations. It is for this reason—that they belong to different spheres of life—that some relations which appear to be independent, are in fact metaphorically associated. The tuning in to the correct resolution of themes is by no means a simple matter, and the realization that the many distinct signals are essentially of the same kind is fundamental. It is the recognition of a common principle, governing seemingly amorphous appearances, which renders the structure coherent.

It has been hinted before that all advertising is regarded as one system, while the different campaigns for specific products are considered as viable sub-systems. It has also been maintained that while the system of appearances of single brands or dominant brands can be further broken down into viable sub-sub-systems, the general campaign for a competitive brand cannot be regarded as a system. Breaking down the system into admissible subsystems, in which the universe of advertisements advocating one product area at a time has been analysed, facilitated the process of decoding. I now wish to reintegrate the fragmented system into a coherent whole and take a look at the structure underlying the great system of appearances of all advertising.

It has been previously perceived that in campaigns which are built around several ECDs, the dimensions, while having an independent existence, tend also to interact with each other. In other words, not only are all the elements reducible to certain ECDs, but also the ECDs, in their turn, enter into certain relations with each other. It must be realized, though, that these relations are coloured by cultural configurations and therefore cannot be claimed to be universal. It is in the sense that the relations outline a map that the recurrent phrase, fundamental dimensions, has been used throughout this work.

The ECDs, or more specifically the signifiers in the ECD, are the dimensions of the structure underlying the whole advertising system. It may be remembered that the ECD is defined as a double sign in which the metaphorical relation between the advertised good and the evoked symbol is like the signified to the signifier, and the same applies to the not-good. Thus, in the analogy formula $A/B = C/D$, two elements in the same structural position (A and C; B and D) constitute a sign, in which A is the signifier of C, and B the signifier of D. The relations between them are metaphorical. On the other hand, the relations between A and B, and C and D are metonymic.[1] We have so far discussed exclusively the metaphorical relations between goods and their evoked images. This chapter is mostly devoted to the implications of the paradigmatic relations between the images themselves.

If the two sides of the ECD are considered separately, two pairs of binary oppositions are obtained, one belonging to the system of goods, or at least to the mental representations of goods, and the other to the repertoire of human ideas. The act of association which brings these two systems together into one super-system, confers on the advertised product the power of the idea evoked, thus creating a symbol. It is in this sense that advertising is an intersection of two communication systems, goods and images, and it is in the ECD that the two systems converge and are super-imposed one upon the other. Because all advertising is reducible to a system of ECDs, which could be split in its turn into a system of symbols, designed to mobilize a system of values, and because the images used make the product more than a product but also a symbol, advertising becomes a centre of communication.

To discuss the structure of all advertising, the analogy drawn between the two types of communication must be left aside for a time while attention is directed to the peculiar relations in the system of images only. This by no means implies that the metaphorical relations are abandoned, but only that in order to pursue the line of reasoning, the specific products considered, as such, no longer matter. It is always possible to supplement the existing structure by drawing the proper analogies, or by constructing a mirror image of the relations in the system of goods, which will faithfully reflect the relations in the system of images.

There is no reason to believe that advertising, unlike other symbolic systems, is controlled by more than a limited number of defining dimensions. It is hard to believe, that while Lévi-Strauss and Edmund Leach have succeeded in demonstrating that this is indeed the case for complex mythological and religious systems, this would not be so for the advertising system.[2] However, rather than striving to discover at this early stage, on the basis of a limited number of representations, what these dimensions may be, I confined myself to the discussion of the criss-crosses which make up the relations among the variables in the system, and which are actually realized in the sample of appearances. Only then may one venture to speculate about the nature of the very few features in terms of which the whole structure can be defined.

Going back to Chapters 3 and 4, the analysed product and not-product categories are signified by the following binary pairs: war/peace, new/old, life/death, in/out (or exogenous/endogenous), body/soul, good/evil, normal/unusual, eternal time/profane time, happiness/misery, knowledge/ignorance, culture/nature, and hot/cold. Already, in this list a certain redundancy is apparent. For instance, in/out, endogenous/exogenous and normal/unusual may be treated not only as redundant, but also as quasi-synonymous expressions. It is fully justifiable to eliminate the internal repetition by selecting only one pair for actual representation in the system. As a rule this kind of repetition was taken care of, so that in the list quoted above, apart from the example given, all obvious redundancy was eliminated in advance. These results are based upon a fairly restricted sample of advertisements. There is no doubt, though, that were I to pursue my investigation further, it would have resulted in ECDs of the same genre. Yet this is not, to my mind, the most interesting outcome. The fact that even within the small confines of the samples used here redundancy among the binary pairs is already manifest seems to be crucial, for it lends support to the view that ultimately the structure of the system rests upon a limited number of controlling dimensions.

I shall proceed by trial and error to place all the binary oppositions, either directly or indirectly, in coherent relations to each other, using only the ones that were obtained as a result of the analysis. Inevitably, this procedure will leave a number of unrelated elements to be completed, which must await further analysis of additional systems of appearances. The system is left open to the introduction of further relations which will undoubtedly modify the present arrangement. The successive arrangements will be continually altered till all the possible relations are introduced, the ultimate positions of all the elements found, and the system made whole. The structural description of Figure 6 could only be understood if the polar oppositions—the relations between which make up the system—are considered in their proper symbolic perspective. It is convenient to start with the binary pair in/out.

It has been maintained before that the universal distinction between the in-group and the out-group is second in importance only to the distinction between ego and alter. Bauman says:

> The same capacity (separation) is operative on the second of the two existentially most fundamental boundaries: this between 'we' and 'they'. We, playing non-zero-sum-game, and they, with whom the zero-sum-game is both inevitable and desirable. We, who share the same fate, who grow rich together or become impoverished together—and they, who prey on our adversities and suffer in case of our success. We, who are expected to

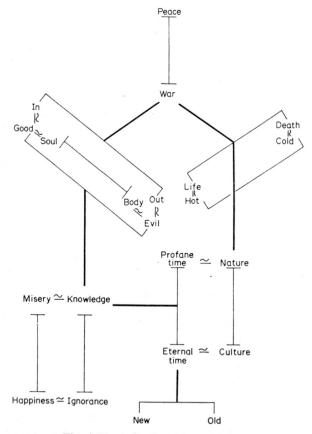

Fig. 6. Towards advertising structure.
Note: the thick lines denote mediation.

assist each other, and they, who lie in wait for our lapse. We, who understand each other, feel the same feelings and think the same thoughts, and they, incomprehensible, impenetrable, unhomely aliens.[3]

The separation between 'we' and 'they' operates on all levels of expression—cosmology, marriage rules, religious affiliations, class distinctions, organizational hierarchies, political movements. 'The sources of it', says Ruth Benedict, 'go far back into what appears to be, from its universal distribution among primitive peoples, one of the earliest of human distinctions, the difference in kind between "my own" closed group and the outsider.'[4]

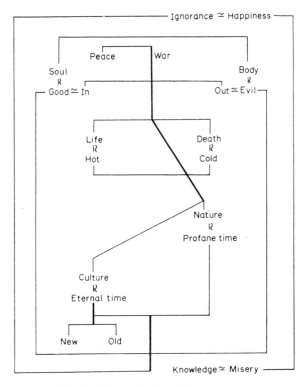

Fig. 6a. Towards advertising structure.
Note: this alternative arrangement is identical with Figure 6. However, while Figure 6 emphasizes the two branches, Figure 6a looks more like an integrated structure.

Leach, pondering on the same phenomenon with regard to marriage rules, claims that the most famous of the endogamy/exogamy rules, that of incest taboo, is based on the separation between 'our kind' (no sexual relations) and 'other kind' with whom sexual relations are permitted. The paradox he points out is rooted in the uncomfortable question: what was the situation at the beginning of time. If the first parents were of two kinds, what was the other kind, and if they were of the same kind then we are all born in sin. 'The myths of the world offer many different solutions to this childish intellectual puzzle, but the prominence which it receives shows that it entails the most profound moral issues . . . If the logic of our thought leads us to distinguish *we* from *they* how can we bridge the gap and establish social and sexual relations with "the others" without throwing our categories into confusion?'[5] That this phenomenon is both universal and operates at all levels of human cognition is further attested to by Eliade, who essentially addresses himself to the cosmogonic implications of this dichotomy: 'At the limits of this closed world begins the domain of the unknown, of the formless. On this side there is ordered—because inhabited and organised—space; on the other, outside this familiar space, there is the unknown and dangerous region of the demons, the ghosts, the dead and the foreigners.'[6]

It is well accepted that the endogenous stands for all that is good, while the exogenous symbolizes all that is evil. One is, thus, permitted to draw the analogy: in : out ≃ good : evil. However, the concepts of good and evil are not only analogous with in and out but also with soul and body. For the body is recognized as the exterior of the soul. While the soul is the gift of God, the body is the source of passion and sin. By the simultaneous distinction of good from evil and body from soul, and by the recognition of body as the shell of the soul, the protection of the soul becomes the sheltering of the in against the out. It is in this sense that the previous analogy could be completed by making body and soul metaphorical with the previous two.

Mary Douglas advances the theory that most symbolic behaviour draws upon body images. In a theory which makes group ('the experience of a bounded social unit') and grid ('the rules which relate one person to others on an ego-centred basis')

the constraining conditions of bodily symbolism, four fundamental possibilities emerge, which affect the nature of the
symbolic system adopted by specific societies.[7] In so far as a
'tendency to express situation of a certain kind in an appropriate
bodily style' is unconscious, and 'in so far as it is obeyed universally in all cultures, the tendency is natural. It is generated in
response to a perceived social situation, but the latter must always
come clothed in its local history and culture. Therefore, the
natural expression is culturally determined.'[8] Without debating
at the moment whether the tendency is culturally determined or
whether, as with all classificatory activity, it originates in the mind,
the important point to notice is that the tendency is universal.

The thick lines in the scheme denote mediation. It will be
realized, that at least in the Judeo-Christian heritage, knowledge
is a mediator between good and evil. The knowledge of the Tree
of Knowledge was a knowledge of good and evil. Moreover,
ignorance and knowledge are equated with happiness and misery.
Knowledge destroyed the blissful paradisical condition, which was
a state of happy ignorance. The way was open to misery as is
symbolized by the Punishment and Fall.[9] Examples of the
relations between as well as the various manifestations of good
and evil, body and soul, knowledge and ignorance, happiness and
misery, abound.[10] I may stop here as it is not my intention to
expound upon symbols which, in themselves, are well known. I
merely wish to point out the implication of having this kind of
relation at the basis of the grand system of advertising.

It may be remembered that I have followed the relationships in
the structure, as it is depicted in Figure 6, by arbitrarily starting
from the binary pair in/out. I have now 'completed' one branch of
relations which are connected with this dimension. It should be
realized that the system had neither a beginning nor an end. Every
pair of oppositions may serve as an arbitrary starting point. The
fact that no element is left unrelated means that all the variables
belong to one network, and that it is this network which endows
them with meaning.

Proceeding to scrutinize the other relations in the system, it
becomes apparent that war/peace constitutes the transformation
channel between the first axis explored above, and the second
branch, which I am about to discuss now. War is a double
mediator. It mediates between in and out, for any war is, by

definition, a clash between we and they, between our kind and their kind. Simultaneously, it is by its very nature a transformation between life and death. Thus, in this schema, war occupies the middle point between the two axes of in/out on the one hand and life/death on the other. Life and death, in its turn, is related to two other themes. To begin with, the analogy between hot/cold and life/death is straightforward. Death is always associated with lack of warmth while life is associated with warmth. This analogy is further extended into other spheres and minutely elaborated in a series of variations all explored in the commercials, such as regeneration/decay, genesis/end, birth/death.

In the set of commercials for brand E, for instance, these themes are particularly strong. When it is considered that the emotional and situational set-up of these commercials is closely attached to agricultural scenes, this proximity is perhaps not very surprising. Thus, according to Eliade 'the drama of vegetation enters into the symbolism of the periodic regeneration of nature and man. Agriculture is only one of the planes upon which the symbolism of periodic regeneration applies. The popular and empiric character of the "agricultural version" of this symbolism has enabled it to attain an extreme dissemination.'[11] And in another place, 'Agricultural divinities took the place of the primitive divinities of the soil, but this substitution did not involve the abolition of all the primeval rites. Underlying the "form" of the agricultural Great Goddesses, we can still detect the presence of the "mistress of the place", the Earth-Mother. But the newer divinities are clearer in feature, more dynamic in their religious structure. There history starts to involve emotion—they *live* the drama of birth, fertility and death.'[12]

Pursuing further the mediating line, it will be realized that in the opposition culture/nature, nature is again a mediator between life and death, a notion which numerous mythologies will attest to. Thus, the belief in autochthony, the idea that man is born from the earth, as well as the great desire at death to return to earth, are ideas of extremely wide currency. Death is a new beginning because it is then that one returns to the eternal womb, the beginning of a new life.[13] The convergence of life and death in nature is the theme of the profound unity of the living and the dead, of man and nature.

The binary pair nature/culture is further positioned in this schema by being metaphorically related to the theme eternal time/profane time. And eternal time/profane time is related, in its turn, to the theme of knowledge/ignorance, which brings us back to the 'first' branch of relations. The link between the latter two pairs is accomplished through a transformation between the profane and the sacred which is analogous to the passage from ignorance to knowledge.

> All the images by means of which we try to express the paradoxical act of 'escaping from time' are equally expressive of the *passage from ignorance to enlightenment* . . . Broadly speaking, they may be grouped into three classes; first, the images that point to the abolition of time, and therefore to enlightenment by *breaking through the planes* . . . Secondly, those that represent an *inconceivable situation* (the Sun standing still in the zenith . . .), and, thirdly and lastly, the contradictory image of the 'favourable moment' a fragment of time transfigured into an 'instant of illumination'. The last two images also suggest a break through the planes, for they symbolise the passage from a normal state at the profane level (the motion of the Sun, the flow of consciousness, etc.), to a paradoxical state (immobility of the Sun, etc.), or imply a transubstantiation taking place within the temporal moment itself.[14]

Indeed the whole of *The Myth of the Eternal Return* is devoted to the significance of sacred and profane time, and the many different forms that the passage between them takes.[15] Finally, the union between new and old expresses continuity and, therefore, it properly belongs to eternal time. Expressed differently, eternal time is the mediator of old and new.

It will be realized that in the schema, as it is conceived of now, while still in an intermediate stage of development, at least one element is left definitely unrelated. That is peace. In a sense the same observation applies to new/old. For though they are related to the other elements through the mediatory power of eternal time, they could be further developed through the formation of other connexions, which at the moment the system does not permit.

The network, as described in Figure 6, is entirely made up of constituent members which have actually appeared in the sample of advertisements. Though there is good reason to believe that the number of fundamental oppositions cannot be very large, it is not assumed that the sample has exhausted the total universe of possibilities. Not knowing the full extent of the system, I do not know whether I am near the completion of the system or not. It is by no means suggested, though, that all that is left to be done is to complete the existing relations. It could well be that further investigation would open up more possibilities or eliminate existing ones rather than just round off the current ones. Future analyses will, no doubt, disclose a high degree of redundancy, as some redundancy is already apparent in the limited sample I have had. At the same time I expect it will reveal the still missing elements. It is only when the missing constituent members are discovered, and the one correct and final arrangement is found, that the structure could be proclaimed complete. It is also expected that then the number of controlling dimensions could be reduced, and the whole system made predictable by the utilization of a few major themes.

Scrutinizing the network in its present rudimentary form, one could speculate about the nature of the controlling dimensions. For in a series of analogies or through mediation some dimensions branch out in more than one direction, and in fact summarize a whole range of possible relations within the boundaries of the existing elements. If such relations continue to hold true when subjected to further modifications, one could argue that they may well be some of the controlling dimensions.

I could have tried to complete the system by deducing what the missing relations may be. While this procedure is perfectly legitimate, and from the point of view of its theoretical neatness rather tempting, it is felt that at this early stage it would be ill-advised. It is premature now to impose upon the system things which seem to be plausible, for future investigation may very well condemn such assumptions as erroneous. It is sufficiently interesting in itself that one could advance a certain way towards the description of a very intricate system simply by adhering to and relying upon the empirical findings. Moreover, as these findings are based on an accidental sample which was determined not by its potential decipherability but by its accessibility, there is every reason to believe that other sub-systems will yield similar results.

So, if it is accepted that advertisements can be generated, given certain rules of combination and transformation, then a system of relations such as the one outlined here may be the overall advertising structure. It has been demonstrated before that for each admissible sub-system, the ECD functions as an exhaustive metaphoric statement or, more specifically, as a structure. Thus one distinguishes here between the specific and homologous manifestations of structures which exhaust the systems of appearances of products; and the overall system of relations which underlie the grand system of all advertising and which is made up of the previously perceived binary relations.

The system of appearances of each product is founded upon the possible permutations of a restricted number of elements which all belong to the same kind. The advertising system is constrained to select its representations from this type of relations alone, and is ultimately bound, in its symbolic function, to the portrayal of several basic themes which are realized in many guises. What Durand says in a different formalistic context applies here too:

> *Ce que la rhétorique peut apporter à la publicité, c'est avant tout une méthode de création. Dans la création publicitaire règne actuellement le mythe de 'l'inspiration', de 'l'idée'. En fait les idées les plus originales, les annonces les plus audacieuses apparaissent comme la transposition de figures de rhétorique répertoriées depuis de nombreux siècles. Cela s'explique puisque la rhétorique est en somme le répertoire des différentes manières par lesquelles on peut être 'original'.*[16]

I have striven to show that symbolic elements of a certain type are bound together in a specified network. This endeavour would have been utterly impossible if it was not for the supposition that a certain classificatory predisposition of the mind has existed a priori. What I did is simply to unveil, in a specific system of appearances, a general tendency which has always been there. This argument does not relate to the genesis of the structure. I do not know how this capacity has evolved. I merely argue that it exists.

In the same way that speech is based on language (in de Saussure), or that individual performance is bound by capacity (in Chomsky), so one may assume that specific representations of symbols and the way in which they are constructed may also be constrained by a certain classificatory predisposition which affects perception in prescribed ways. 'It is difficult to avoid the conclusion', says Chomsky, 'that whatever its function may be, the reliance on structure-dependent operations must be predetermined for the language-learner by a restrictive initial schematism of some sort that directs his attempts to acquire linguistic competence.'[17] Chomsky is not alone in his conviction. Linguists, such as Fodor, Katz and others share his views.[18] And the biologist, Lennenberg, provides a fascinating analysis of the biological foundations of language, in support of the conclusion concerning innate structures.[19] In a similar vein Piaget discusses the innate roots of behaviour, and the predetermined stages of the development from reflex-complexes through acquired habits to sensory-motor and intelligence. All such behaviour stems from an innate predisposition and becomes differentiated through functioning. Nevertheless it contains the same functional factors ('assimilation' and 'accommodation') and the same structural elements. The structural elements are, in brief, certain 'order relations', 'sub-ordination schemes' and 'correspondences'.[20] Chomsky argues, on the basis of the findings of Mehler and Bever, for a stronger assumption than Piaget's. The results of these studies suggest, according to Chomsky, that conservation may not demonstrate successive stages of intellectual development, but rather 'that the "final stage" in which conservation is properly understood, was already realised at a very early period of development . . . If this analysis is correct, then what we are observing is not a succession of stages of intellectual development, in Piaget's sense, but rather slow progress in bringing heuristic techniques into line with general concepts that have always been present.'[21] Already Gestalt psychologists have argued that perception is not random but subjected to certain fixed laws.[22] Current research in physio-logical psychology, and especially the work of Bower, suggests that the perceptual constancies are based on innate mechanism.[23] It is concluded, then, 'that perception of line, angle, motion, and other complex properties of the physical world is based on innate organisation of the neural system.'[24] Maslow, working in a field quite remote from the previous ones, seems to argue that even the basic needs, in his understanding of the term, conform to a specific predetermined innate hierarchy. The basic needs, by order of potency, are: physiological needs, safety needs, love needs, esteem needs and self-actualization needs.[25] 'Our main hypothesis is', says Maslow, 'that human *urges* or *basic needs* alone may be innately given to at least some appreciable degree . . . the basic needs stand in a special psychological and biological status. There is something different about them. The burden of proof that they are not appreciably instinctoid rests upon anyone who denies this.'[26]

There is, as I have briefly indicated above, a growing body of knowledge which seems to suggest that innate species-specific characteristics are at the root of much of human behaviour which previously was attributed to such external mechanisms as culture and society. One may venture to conclude, as others seem to do, and as Lévi-Strauss actually demonstrates in practice, that the symbolic function is embedded in the mind and is constrained by certain given schemata. Lévi-Strauss goes even further than that. Symbols are defined, in a way which is perfectly congruent with the sense in which they are employed here, to be 'meaningful equivalents of things meant which belong to another order of reality.'[27] For him, the symbolic function is structured according to the laws of the unconscious.

The unconscious in structuralist theory is neither a reservoir of private repressed recollections and ideas; nor a set of collective primordial images, as it is for Jung. The structuralist unconscious is an innate structure, or rather a set of a priori given structuring rules, which imposes its laws upon human mental activity, of which language acquisition and the capacity for symbolization, are but two prominent examples. Some structuralists, Lacan for example, go even further than that to pinpoint the nature of the unconscious. In his most striking conclusion, he maintains that the structure of the unconscious is the structure of language.[28]

Structuralism owes much to Freud. It is from him that it borrows the conception of the unconscious as an existing all-encompassing yet unapprehended reality. Moreover, Freud, much in the spirit as contemporary structuralists, attempts to formulate laws of transformation between the unconscious and the conscious mind. It is from him, that the full realization of the true nature of the unconscious, as a latent *mental category* which governs much of our psychic life, is borrowed.[29] And the idea that conscious models screen the true apprehension of things, which is the basic theme of *The Interpretation of Dreams*, is again eminently Freudian.[30] It is in his analysis of dreams that Freud outlines the general rules of the unconscious. And this choice was not a mere chance, for dreams follow the same laws in the normal and the neurotic.

Jung, on the other hand, is much scorned by the structuralist school. Though the structuralist conception of the unconscious is collective, like Jung's, this is the limit of the resemblance. For Jung addresses himself to the contents of the unconscious and regards them as both collective and universal, while the structuralist views content as being always infinitely varied, and therefore specific. The only reality which is collective and, therefore, universal, is form. In other words, the structuring laws of the human mind are universal, not the specific contents in which they are expressed.

It is interesting to note that Jung came close in some respects to this view. In *The Archetypes and the Collective Unconscious* he says: 'There are as many archetypes as there are typical situations in life. Endless repetition has engraved these experiences into our psychic constitution, not in the form of images filled with content, but at first only as *forms without content*, representing merely the possibility of a certain type of perception and action.'[31] Later in the book he reaches his final verdict on the situation:

> Again and again I encounter the mistaken notion that an archetype is determined in regard to its content, in other words that it is a kind of unconscious idea (if such an expression be admissible). It is necessary to point out once more that archetypes are not determined as regards their content, but only as regards their form and then only to a very limited degree. A primordial image is determined as to its content only when it has become conscious and is therefore filled out with the material of conscious experience . . . The archetype in itself is empty and purely formal, nothing but a *facultas praeformandi*, a possibility of representation which is given *a priori*. The representations themselves are not inherited, only the forms, and in that respect they correspond in every way to the instincts, which are also determined in form only.[32]

Jung was only too well aware of the distinction between form and content. Indeed he laboured to emphasize that his archetypes are forms only. It is therefore not so much in his conception of content against form as in his application of these notions that Jung deviates from the structuralist perspective.[33] For in his actual exposition of the archetypes, is the discussion of contents.[34] However, the point which makes the theories unbridgeable is his insistence on discussing the elements in isolation and his failure to realize that a few structural laws underlie the whole symbolic function. Moreover, in his view it is not the system of relations which endow any specific element with meaning, but the meaning is intrinsic to the element itself. In summary then, the structuralist school, and particularly Lévi-Strauss, maintain:

The unconscious ceases to be the ultimate haven of individual peculiarities—the repository of a unique history which makes each of us an irreplaceable being. It is reducible to a function— the symbolic function, which no doubt is specifically human, and which is carried out according to the same laws among all men, and actually corresponds to the aggregate of these laws ... The unconscious ... is always empty—or, more accurately, it is as alien to mental images as is the stomach to the foods which pass through it. As the organ of a specific function, the unconscious merely imposes structural laws upon inarticulated elements which originate elsewhere—impulses, emotions, representations, and memories ... If we add that these structures are not only the same for everyone and for all areas to which the function applies, but that they are few in number, we shall understand why the world of symbolism is infinitely varied in content, but always limited in its laws.[35]

I have concerned myself so far with the way in which systems of appearances may be reduced to a structural resolution of themes. It has been further realized that these specific structural resolutions are but fragments of relations which constitute parts of a much larger and intricate network. I have then proceeded to investigate the nature of this system, as far as the advertising activity is concerned. Yet may one not ask at this stage whether these binary relations do not also have another significance which, though implied in everything I have said so far, has never been explicitly stated? Is not this network of oppositions which underly the advertising system nothing else but a system of universal polarities or, if one so prefers, a set of binary archetypes? And finally, is it not possible to conclude that the advertising system, as other symbolic systems, possesses more than a superficial resemblance to another and more perfect expression of the human mind, namely to myth?

The evidence of Chapters 3 and 4 suggests that advertising is constructed like myth. They both obey the same laws of composition, and they are both structured in the same manner. In other words, the mental operation involved, the process of coding and decoding, is identical. It is this theme of profound unity between the archaic and the contemporary, between the seemingly disparate, which has proved to be a source of constant fascination to me in this work. The process of classification and the imposition of order on a random reality is always the same, though the specific manifestations of the same fundamental laws differ. In so far as the universality of the symbolic function is accepted, advertising is but one variation of this perpetual and universal underlying pattern. It is not merely that advertising shares with myth some such common themes, as Cinderella or the chasing satyr. This is the least of it. The most significant aspect of the comparison is that both advertising and myth obey the same laws of construction and the same rules of order and classification. That advertising structure is simpler than that of myth is but a reflection of the fact that advertising is a degenerated form of myth. For one thing it is poorer in detail, and for another it lacks, particularly in static advertising, the temporal dimension.

It is a point of great interest that besides the astonishing similarity in the manner in which these two symbolic productions behave, they are also preoccupied with essentially the same problems. Both strive to provide answers to the eternal polarities of the human condition. While the dichotomies, or the dilemmas, are universal, the specific answers are not. The resolution of theme in the analysis is universal, in the sense that all people, wherever they may be, must wrestle with the same fundamental problems of life/death, we/they, war/peace, happiness/misery, and so on. The specific relations among binary pairs, however, are coloured by the special flavour of the particular cultural enclosure in which they operate. The classificatory activity of the mind alone is both predetermined and universal. But the specific configurations of relationships between variables are culturally bound. The essential point is that the human mind is sensitive to certain problems which emanate from the human condition and are specific to the human species. These problems are universally apprehended and as such constitute universal themes. The specific solutions offered to them are, nevertheless, varied.

To the recurrent question in Eliade's writings: 'what has become of myth in the modern world?'; or more precisely, 'what has taken the essential place occupied by the myth in traditional societies?'[36]—to this I advance the answer that myth is disguised in advertising. An answer which, indeed, is not far removed from Eliade's own speculations: 'some forms of "mythical behaviour" still survive in our day. This does not mean that they represent "survivals" of an archaic mentality. But certain aspects and functions of mythical thought are constituents of the human being.'[37] He is convinced that myth has never disappeared from modern life, but has only taken on a different form. Moreover, myth is concealed in the most ordinary manifestations of everyday life.[38] The central position of myth is filled, in contemporary society, by the comics, detective stories, superman, public figures and even the education system.[39] The essential structure of myth survives, though in a corrupted and a degraded form.[40]

If advertising is said to be a modern myth, what other evidence could one offer in support of such a contention? It has been previously concluded that advertising masters a number of basic roles. It mediates between the abstract and the concrete, as well as between social values, cultural symbols and ordinary everyday consumption behaviour. Further, it is a communication process and an intersection of at least two major types of communication: that of signs and that of values. In other words, it uses the dialogue of signs to effect the exchange of values. It has also been demonstrated that advertising has two faces: a surface manifestation with which everyone is familiar, and a second, hidden level which underlies the surface representations and endows it with meaning. Yet this 'other' message is not immediately apparent and is rarely decodable from a single appearance. To be able to unveil the underlying structure, the diverse appearances must constitute a system. It is the message of the system in toto which is different from the private messages of each isolated representation.

Advertising shares with myth a number of features. They are both integrated systems and they both share a structure and basic themes. Advertising, particularly dynamic advertising, has, like myth, a synchronic as well as a diachronic aspect. Each product is illustrated by many different versions as each mythical story has many variations. They are both repetitive.

But if advertising is indeed a myth in modern disguise, then it also has the same role in modern societies as the myth has in traditional societies. Lévi-Strauss defines this role as being the resolution of contradictions. Myths reinforce accepted behaviour by scanning all the alternative solutions and 'proving' that the one which predominates is, in any society, in given circumstances, the best. As such, the myth is precisely like advertising—a conservative force. It is not concerned with revolutionizing the existing order of things, but in preserving it.

Over and beyond this, advertising (like a myth) acts as an anxiety-reducing mechanism. It does this, first, by restating essential dilemmas of the human condition and, second, by offering a solution to them. To the constant nagging dilemmas of life, advertising gives a simple answer. In buying certain products or obtaining a service, one buys not only a 'thing', but also an image. This image consists of the belief and the hope in something better. The general argument runs something like this: If the advertised product is purchased, one will belong rather than be excluded, one will have happiness rather than misery, good rather than evil, life rather than death. Advertising simultaneously provokes anxiety and resolves it.

Finally, in the same manner that myth is an expression of a certain mode of symbolic perception to people in certain types of society, so is advertising eminently suitable to play this role in modern, industrialized, commercialized society. No society exists without some form of myth. Once this is realized, it is not very surprising that a society which is based on the economy of mass production and mass consumption will evolve its own myth in the form of the commercial. Like myth it touches upon every facet of life, and as a myth it makes use of the fabulous in its application to the mundane. Yet in neither do people stop to say, 'but this is impossible'.

I have come to the end of my tale of advertising. I have striven to test one major hypothesis which stipulates the existence of an underlying structure to which all advertising appearances are reducible. This stipulation has been borne out. I have then pursued some of the logical and practical implications of the decodability of advertising into a structure, and advanced some suggestions concerning the nature of the advertising activity. As two chapters have been devoted to these implications any additional summarizing would be redundant.

It is clear, though, that many problems remain unsolved. One does not know what role the product itself plays, if at all, in the advertising system. Is it just an unimportant appendage, or are there some fundamental relations between the structural theme and the advocated thing, so that some themes are intrinsically better suited to some specific products? Is there a grand system effect on perception? In other words, how do the binary pairs interact with each other? Are there some consonant or alternatively dissonant relations? If so, how does this affect perception? Would specific resolutions of themes of specific product areas repeat themselves across language and cultural frontiers, e.g. is detergent advertising always based on good and evil, and baby foods on life and death? Is it possible to establish a co-ordinated system of rules which will be the language of advertising? If the underlying message influences behaviour, is it possible to sell whatever kind of product one chooses, provided that the right structures are evoked? Can one devise a system of transformation laws which would allow one to travel back from the deep structure to the surface manifestations, in other words, to generate advertisements?

Many more questions may be asked, but I will stop here. Some speculations concerning these issues have been offered in the course of this study. Others are destined, at least for the time being, to remain a mystery.

References

1. E. K. Maranda, 'The logic of riddles', in P. Maranda and E. K. Maranda, eds, *Structural Analysis of Oral Tradition* (Philadelphia: University of Pennsylvania Press, 1971), pp. 193–4.
2. See, for instance, the discussion of the traffic triangle, the culinary triangle and the phonological triangle, in E. Leach, *Lévi-Strauss* (Fontana, 1970), pp. 24–35; also the structural analysis of the Greek mythology in the same book, pp. 66–82. See also, E. Leach, 'The Legitimacy of Solomon', in *Genesis as a Myth* (Cape Editions, 1969), pp. 25–84.
3. Z. Bauman, *Culture as Praxis* (Routledge & Kegan Paul, 1973).
4. R. Benedict, *Patterns of Culture* (Routledge & Kegan Paul, 1935), p. 5.
5. E. Leach, *Genesis as a Myth*, pp. 10–11.

6. M. Eliade, *Images and Symbols* (Harvill Press, 1952), pp. 37–8.

7. M. Douglas, *Natural Symbols* (Barrie & Jenkins, 1970).

8. Ibid., p. 69.

9. See in J. M. Kitagawa and C. H. Long, eds, *Myths and Symbols* (Chicago: University of Chicago Press, 1969), a paper by G. Scholem, particularly p. 165.

10. See, for instance, M. Douglas, *Natural Symbols*; Douglas, *Witchcraft, Confessions and Accusations* (Tavistock Publications, 1970); G. Zunini, *Man and His Religion* (Geoffrey Chapman, 1969); J. M. Yinger, *Religion, Society and the Individual* (New York: The Macmillan Co., 1957); M. Weber, *The Protestant Ethic and the Spirit of Capitalism* (Allen & Unwin, 1930); E. Leach, *Genesis as a Myth*; P. L. Berger, *The Social Reality of Religion* (Faber, 1969); J. Middleton, ed., *Myth and Cosmos* (New York: The Natural History Press, 1967); M. Eliade, *Shamanism* (Routledge & Kegan Paul, 1964); Eliade, *Myth and Reality* (Allen & Unwin, 1964); 'Myth de combat et de repos dyades et polarites' in *Eranos-Jahrbuch*, vol. 36 (1968), pp. 59–111; E. Durkheim and M. Mauss, *Primitive Classifications* (Cohen & West, 1963); E. Neumann, *The Great Mother* (Routledge & Kegan Paul, 1955).

11. M. Eliade, *The Myth of the Eternal Return* (Routledge & Kegan Paul, 1955), p. 64.

12. M. Eliade, *Patterns in Comparative Religion* (Sheed & Ward, 1958), p. 261.

13. M. Eliade, *The Sacred and the Profane* (New York: Harper Torch Books, Harper & Row, 1957), p. 157; *Myths, Dreams and Mysteries* (New York: Harper Torch Books, Harper & Row, 1957), p. 165.

14. M. Eliade, *Images and Symbols*, pp. 82–3.

15. M. Eliade, *The Myth of the Eternal Return*.

16. J. Durand, 'Rhétoriques et image publicitaire', *Communications*, no. 15 (1970), p. 91.

17. N. Chomsky, *Language and Mind* (New York: Harcourt, Brace & World, 1968), p. 52.

18. J. A. Fodor and J. J. Katz, eds, *The Structure of Language* (New Jersey: Prentice Hall, 1964); J. J. Katz, *The Philosophy of Language* (Harper & Row, 1966); J. Lyons, ed., *New Horizons in Linguistics* (Penguin Books, 1970); R. C. Oldfield and J. C. Marshall, eds, *Language* (Penguin Books, 1968).

19. E. H. Lennenberg, 'The capacity for language acquisition' in J. A. Fodor and J. J. Katz, eds, *The Structure of Language*, pp. 579–603; E. H. Lennenberg, ed., *New Directions in the Study of Language* (New York: John Wiley, 1967); for a different point of view, see B. L. Whorf, *Language, Thought, and Reality* (Cambridge, Mass: M.I.T. Press, 1956); A. Koestler, *The Ghost in the Machine* (Pan Books, 1967).

20. J. Piaget, *Structuralism* (Routledge & Kegan Paul, 1971). Particularly relevant is his chapter IV: 'Psychological structures', p. 63; also, I. E. Sigel and F. H. Hooper, eds, *Logical Thinking in Children* (Holt, Rinehart and Winston, 1968).

21. N. Chomsky, *Language and Mind*, p. 80; 'Problems of explanation in

linguistics' in R. Borger and F. Cioffi, *Explanations in the Behavioral Sciences* (Cambridge University Press, 1970).

22. J. Piaget, *Structuralism*, pp. 54–60.
23. N. Chomsky, *Language and Mind*, p. 80.
24. Ibid.
25. A. H. Maslow, *Motivation and Personality* (New York: Harper & Row, 1954); in particular Ch. 5; also, *Toward a Psychology of Being*, 2nd ed. (van Nostrand, 1968).
26. Ibid., pp. 141–2.
27. C. Lévi-Strauss, *Structural Anthropology* (Allen Lane, The Penguin Press, 1968), p. 200.
28. See J. Lacan, *Ecrits*; also, J. M. Auzias, *Clefs pour le structuralisme* (Paris: Seghers, 1971), pp. 147–83; and Yale French Studies, *Structuralism* (1966), particularly papers by J. Miel and J. Lacan.
29. Sigmund Freud, in particular 'A note on the unconscious in psychoanalysis', pp. 22–9, 'The unconscious', pp. 98–136, in *Collected Papers*, vol. IV (Hogarth Press, 1956).
30. Sigmund Freud, *The Interpretation of Dreams* (Allen & Unwin, 1954), pp. 610–21; see also Sigmund Freud, *Totem and Taboo* (Routledge & Kegan Paul, 1958).
31. C. G. Jung, *The Archetypes and the Collective Unconscious* (Routledge & Kegan Paul, 1959), p. 48.
32. Ibid., p. 79.
33. See for example, ibid., p. 70, on binary oppositions.
34. C. G. Jung and C. Kerényi, *Introduction to the Science of Mythology* (Routledge & Kegan Paul, 1951); C. G. Jung, *The Structure and Dynamics of the Psyche* (Routledge & Kegan Paul, 1960); Jung, *Four Archetypes* (Routledge & Kegan Paul, 1972); Jung, *The Interpretation and Nature of the Psyche* (Routledge & Kegan Paul, 1955); Jung, *Psychological Reflections* (Routledge & Kegan Paul, 1961); Jung, *Memories, Dreams, Reflections* (Collins and Routledge, 1963).
35. C. Lévi-Strauss, *Structural Anthropology*, pp. 202–3.
36. M. Eliade, *Myths, Dreams and Mysteries*, p. 24.
37. M. Eliade, 'Survivals and camouflages of myth', *Diogenes*, no. 41 (1963), pp. 18–19; see also Eliade, 'The prestige of the cosmogonic myth', *Diogenes*, no. 23 (Fall, 1958), pp. 1–13; J. Ellul, 'Modern myths', *Diogenes*, no. 23 (Fall, 1958), pp. 23–40.
38. M. Eliade, *Images and Symbols*, pp. 18–19.
39. M. Eliade, 'Survivals and camouflages of myth', op. cit., pp. 19–20; also, D. G. MacRae, 'Advertising and social structure', in *Advertising Quarterly*, vol. 1, no. 1 (August, 1964); MacRae, *Ideology and Society* (Heinemann, 1961), pp. 77–86.
40. M. Eliade, *Myths, Dreams and Mysteries*, pp. 27–8; Eliade, *Patterns in Comparative Religion*, pp. 431–2; T. A. Sebeok, *Myth,* a symposium (Bloomington, Ind: Indiana University Press, 1958).

Appendix I. Brand A (BA)
advertisements

1. 'Here's a nice clean shirt.' 'Thanks.' 'It's quite clean—shame it looks so dull!' 'Dull!'
'Dull!'
'Can you do better?' 'You could—use this new power BA.' 'I could!'
'Yes.'
New power BA boosts white clean through to bright—go on try it. New power BA has all the power to get your wash clean and white—of course it has—but it doesn't stop at clean and white, it goes on to boost white through to bright. There—that shirt isn't dull any more, its clean and white and really bright and that goes for the rest of your wash too. Sheets look zingier, skirts look swingier, even overalls look, well, zippier. Now your whole wash is so much brighter.
'Fantastic.'
Get blue power BA. Blue power BA boosts white clear through to bright.

2. This is a giant-size pack of BA and this $\frac{1}{2}$lb is free. Yes, you get $\frac{1}{2}$lb free in giant-size BA and there's a $\frac{1}{4}$lb free in the large size too.

3. Here's a Christmas present from BA to you—these beautiful table glasses in four tested colours to brighten your Christmas table, free with BA. Take two with family size, one with giant. Collect a set for Christmas.

4. Hmmm, steak pie for tea—Jim's favourite. This pie-dish makes a really man-size pie and it's free with giant BA—so do buy BA and collect these free pie-dishes at your grocers now.

5. Look! Free with BA—fine quality table glasses in lilac, meadow green, smoke blue, or amber. Help yourself to a glass with every BA giant pack. Collect a set—they're free with BA.

6. No it isn't Christmas, its BA free gift time again. There are five fabulous BA gifts and here they are:

   a vacuum flask with special leak-proof seal;
   an insulated Polytemp mug;
   an oven-proof Pyrex bowl, guaranteed one year;
   a good, big food-box, ideal for storage; and
   a gaily coloured cotton teatowel from Portugal.

   All these wonderful gifts are free from BA. Collect BA packet tops and send away for your free gifts now.

7. Times change—it's a bright new world.
   ("Bye, Mummy')
   But clothes still get dirty. Very dirty.
   (Traffic noises, etc.)
   Time we did something about it—new BA does.
   It gets tough—BA has changed. Suddenly new BA has bright new power, concentrated power, power to beat dirt, to shift stains, bright new power to whiten right through the wash. You want it that way. You want your things cleaner, whiter, more than that—brighter. You feel brighter—you are brighter. New BA gets tough, really tough, with bright new power for a bright new world.

8. Suddenly there's bright new power in BA and you get $\frac{1}{2}$lb free in every special giant pack, a free $\frac{1}{2}$lb and bright new power in every special giant pack of BA now.

9. Suddenly there's bright new power in BA and you get $\frac{1}{2}$lb free in every special giant pack and a free $\frac{1}{4}$lb in the special large pack. Try the bright new power of BA now.

10. Times change. It's a bright new world.
    ('No fighting')
    But clothes still get dirty. Very dirty.

Time we did something about it. New BA does.

It gets tough. BA has changed. Suddenly new BA has bright new power, concentrated power, power to beat dirt, to shift stains, bright new power to whiten right through the wash. You want it that way. You want things cleaner, whiter, more than that, brighter. You feel brighter. You are brighter. New BA gets tough, really tough with bright new power for a bright new world.

11. Roll up, this is the BA Summer Fair, with free gifts for everyone.
'. . . and what about this lovely tray, this pastry server, a measuring jug, unbreakable, or these beautiful French glass fruit bowls and all free in the one and only BA Summer Fair.' All you do is collect BA packet tops and the gifts are yours ladies. Follow the details on the BA Summer Fair pack.

12. Times change—its a bright new world.
("Bye, Mummy')
But clothes still get dirty. Very dirty.
Time we did something about it. New BA does.
It gets tough. BA has changed. Suddenly new BA has bright new power, concentrated power, power to beat dirt, to shift stains, bright new power to whiten right through the wash, you want it that way. You want your things cleaner, whiter, more than that, brighter. You feel brighter, you are brighter. New BA gets tough, really tough, with bright new power for a bright new world.

13. Suddenly there's bright new power in BA and you get a $\frac{1}{4}$lb free in every special giant pack. A free $\frac{1}{4}$lb of bright new power in every special giant pack of BA, now.

14. Now you have the power—you and your family. The bright new power of BA, unbeatable power to shift stains, unbeatable power to shift dirt, unbeatable power to whiten right through the wash. Bright new power for a bright new world.

15. Here's a bright new way to collect bright new cups and saucers. They're free from BA. With every special giant pack

you get a free cup or saucer in bright new colours. So buy giant BA and get a free cup or saucer.

16. Here's a bright new way to collect bright new cups and saucers. They're free from BA. With every special giant pack you get a free cup or saucer in bright new colours and that's not all—here's an extra bargain—a BA sale. Matching cup, saucer and plate—2/6d. a set. Send for as many sets as you like. And remember this special giant BA packet starts you off with a free cup or saucer.

17. Now you have the power. You and your family. The bright new power of BA. Unbeatable power to shift stains, unbeatable power to shift dirt, unbeatable power to whiten right through the wash. Bright new power for a bright new world.

18. Now you have the power. You and your family. The bright new power of BA. Unbeatable power to shift stains, unbeatable power to shift dirt, unbeatable power to whiten right through the wash. Bright new power for a bright new world.

19. Now you have the power. For you and your family. The bright new power of BA. More power to shift stains, more power to shift dirt, more power to whiten right through the wash. Bright new power for a bright new world.

20. Now you have the power, for you and your family. The bright new power of BA, more power to shift stains, more power to shift dirt, more power to whiten right through the wash. Bright new power for a bright new world.

21. Now you have the power, for you and your family. The bright new power of BA, more power to shift stains, more power to shift dirt, more power to whiten right through the wash. Bright new power for a bright new world.

22. To help you cope with this bright new world, ('Hopeless, you'll never get it finished')

brighter, faster, more demanding than ever,
('Hello, Hello')
to help you BA now increases its bright new power. New BA
—more power than ever before, stain removal power, more
power and more brightness. Much more brightness for
cleaner, whiter, brighter clothes—to help you cope, new BA,
now even more power, even more brightness.

23. To help you cope with this bright new world,
   ("Bye') ('Hey, Harry, bring that jeep . . .') brighter, faster,
   more demanding than ever. ('If your father could see you')
   To help you, BA now increases its bright new power. New
   BA—more power than ever before, stain removal power,
   more power and more brightness. Much more brightness for
   cleaner, whiter, brighter clothes to help you cope, new
   BA—now even more power, even more brightness.

24. To help you cope with this bright new world—brighter,
   faster, more demanding than ever. ('Jenny') ('Hmm well no')
   ('Look at that shirt') To help you, BA now increases its
   bright new power. New BA—more power than ever before,
   stain removal power, more power and more brightness. Much
   more brightness for cleaner, whiter, brighter clothes. To
   help you cope, new BA—now even more power, even more
   brightness.

25. Stand by for an important announcement about stains, the
   ones a normal wash won't get out completely, like tea, red
   wine, blackberry—now; they'll shift with BA. New BA has a
   new power trigger called T. T BA in five minutes washes out
   stains that only special treatment could lift out before, the
   unshiftables. In new T BA the unshiftables shift. In an
   ordinary washer—any age—in five minutes red wine, tea,
   blackberry—stains no washing power could shift in a five
   minutes wash before, new T BA eliminates completely. You
   don't have to soak them first. In new T BA the unshiftables
   shift.

26. The stuff in this packet, in a normal wash, in an ordinary
   washer like this—not your automatics—just an ordinary

machine, will get clothes cleaner in five minutes than all the other washing products put together. I'll tell you something else, in that five minutes it will wash out stains that only special treatment could lift before. A larger number of stains than any other powder you care to name. This packet is BA— a new BA—new and even better. T BA—the power trigger called T makes BA so powerful, in a normal wash, that it shifts some stains that even those new soak and wash products find unshiftable, like red wine, tea, blackberry. T BA shifts them without any soaking in five minutes. One wash with new T BA and it looks as if you've got yourself a new washing machine.

27. Your bright new world. Brighter, faster, tougher, ('Hopeless, you'll never get it finished') tougher on clothes too. To help you cope BA now increases its bright new power, power to soak, more power to shift stains in the wash—and with more power much more brightness. For cleaner, whiter, brighter clothes to help you cope, new BA, now even more power, even more brightness.

28. Your bright new world. ("Bye') ('Hey, Harry, bring that jeep') brighter, faster ('Let's go') tougher on clothes too. ('If your father could see you.') To help you cope, BA now increases its brightening power, power to soak, more power to shift stains in the wash and with more power much more brightness. For cleaner, whiter, brighter clothes to help you cope—new BA—now even more power, even more brightness.

29. Your bright new world. Brighter, faster, tougher ('Jenny') tougher on clothes too ('Look at that shirt!') To help you cope BA now increases its bright new power, power to soak, more power to shift stains in the wash and with more power, much more brightness. For cleaner, whiter, brighter clothes to help you cope new BA—now even more power, even more brightness.

30. In this bright new world when there's no time to soak, no time to bleach, the washing powder you need must be fast

and it must be here—where BA's got it—in the wash. Cleaning power in the wash, stain removal power in the wash, BA brightening power in the wash. With BA you get your clothes clean, white and bright and you get it fast. BA power, where you need it, in the wash.

31. Stand by for an important announcement about stains, the ones a normal wash won't get out completely, the un-shiftables like tea, blackberry, red wine—now they'll shift with BA. New BA with a new power agent called T. In five minutes in an ordinary washer T BA washes out stains only special treatment could lift before—tea, blackberry, red wine. Stains no five minutes washing could shift until now, new T BA eliminates completely. No need to soak; in new T BA unshiftables shift.

32. Some stains happen now and then. Some keep on happening —the stains you get simply from living—perspiration, blood, the understains. The most difficult even to talk about. New biological BA has now put an end to the understains. This new biological formula is strong enough in the soak to break the hold of blood, perspiration, understains. New BA—so much stronger on stains—it has to be brighter. It is brighter. A cleaner, fresher, brighter BA, stronger on stains, brighter on brightness. New biological BA.

33. Last year Lucy Lambert opened 1312 cans.
'Ah, Mrs Lambert, here's just what you need, a wall can opener by Prestige and BA is giving away 100 000 of them. All you do is send four BA packet tops from any giant-size packet to this address—think of it, a free can opener.' 'Oh, I could do this all day.' 'Look, here's the BA, why not get your own can opener.'

34. Last year Lucy Lambert opened 1312 cans.
'Ah, Mrs Lambert, here's just what you need, a wall can opener by Prestige and BA is giving away 100 000 of them. All you do is send four BA packet tops from any giant-size packet to this address—think of it, a free can opener.' 'Oh, I

could do this all day.' 'Look, here's the BA, why not get your own can opener.'

35. They are the stains you get simply from living—perspiration, blood, the understains. The most difficult even to talk about. New biological BA is strong enough in the soak to break the hold of blood, perspiration, understains.
The new BA—so much stronger on stains, it has to be brighter. A fresh, clean, bright start with new biological BA.

36. These are the most difficult stains—the stains you get simply from living. 'Come on then, there's a good boy.' Perspiration, blood, the understains, the most difficult even to talk about. New biological BA overpowers the understains with a new biological formula. Strong enough in the soak to break the hold of blood, perspiration, understains. A new BA, so much stronger on stains it has to be brighter. A fresh, clean, bright start every day. Brighter on brightness, because it's stronger on stains. New biological BA.

37. They are the stains you get simply from living. Perspiration, blood, the understains, the most difficult even to talk about. New biological BA is strong enough on the soak to break the hold of blood, perspiration, understains. A new BA, so much stronger on stains it has to be brighter. A fresh, clean, bright start with new biological BA.

38. They are the stains you get simply from living. Perspiration, blood, the understains, the most difficult even to talk about. New biological BA is strong enough in the soak to break the hold of blood, perspiration, understains. The new BA, so much stronger on stains it has to be brighter. A fresh, clean, bright start with new biological BA.

39. They are the stains you get simply from living. Perspiration, blood, the understains, the most difficult even to talk about. New biological BA is strong enough in the soak to break the hold of blood, perspiration, understains. The new BA, so much stronger on stains it has to be brighter. A fresh, clean, bright start with new biological BA.

40. They are the stains you get simply from living. Perspiration, blood, the understains, the most difficult even to talk about. New biological BA is expressly made to break the hold of blood, perspiration, the understains. Washing that's free of understains has to be fresh and clean again. That's what biological BA is about.

Appendix II. Brand B (BB) advertisements

1. 'This is new energy BB with nearly three times more washing power to wash out stains, it washes much whiter. But do housewives agree? Hello Mrs Kent.'
'Hello.'
'Another busy washday I see.'
'Yes.'
'Tell me about what's here?'
'Ah, my sheet I washed in BB has come up lovely and white as you can see. Look—and this tablecloth here was grey and has come up a hundred per cent, all the stains have come out since I've used BB.'
'Very good indeed. How many children have you got Mrs Kent?'
'I've got five children.'
'Big family.'
'Yes.'
'You have a lot of washing to do have you?'
'I should say that.'
'Well laugh at that.' (She laughs.) 'That's it, lovely, right.'
'This coloured piece here is my husband's—a lorry driver.'
'What sort of stains do you get on it?'
'Grease on it and as you can see all the stains have come out, all the grease stains have come up really white.'
'What do you think of new BB?'
'Well I think it's great, it's fabulous.'
'It's great. It's fabulous. New BB, with nearly three times more power to drive out stains, washes much whiter. In fact no other powder, soap or detergent can wash whiter. Try it.'

2. (Background noise.)

'Now ladies, to give the Hoovermatic a real test, let's wash the things you've brought in.'

'Oh Mary, this isn't Sam's old garden shirt.'

'It is.'

'Even you couldn't get that really white now.'

'Nor will they.'

'Now first we have a towel here and then . . .'

'Tell me, why BB?'

'Because Hoover recommends it. BB has exclusive active blueing and that means a difference in whiteness, as you'll see.'

'Now, which two ladies gave white shirts?'

'That's mine.'

'Here what a difference!'

'Then this must be yours?'

'Never.'

'It is, Mary, look at the label.'

'I'm flabbergasted.'

'Why?'

'The white, it's unbelievable.'

'Oh that's the exclusive active blueing in BB; it means a difference in whiteness you can see. Now you know why Hoover recommend BB and no other detergent.'

'He'll not wear this shirt gardening again!' (Laughter.)

3. 'New energy BB washes whiter, that's what all these Cornish housewives found. Among them, Mrs Atkins. What do you think of new energy BB?'

'Oh I'm very pleased with it indeed. My husband's shirt has come up beautifully and white.'

'What does your husband do for a living?'

'We own a snack bar.'

'That's a dirty job is it?'

'Well tea-cloths especially, because we use about a dozen a day and they do get badly stained you know, but they've come up beautifully and white.'

'Would you say that new BB gets rid of stains?'

'Well it does, I hadn't . . . well all the washing I've done, I can honestly say that every stain's removed from every bit I've washed. That's my tablecloth. I'm very pleased it's beautiful

and white 'cos with a big place like mine there's always tea stains, treacle, jam, tea upset and I'm really pleased, it is really white. Whitest I've ever seen it.'
'Test it yourself and see. No other powder, soap or detergent can wash whiter than new energy BB.'

4. 'A major breakthrough for washing machine owners. New energy BB. It washes much whiter. In fact, no other powder, soap or detergent can wash whiter. But we asked Philips to see what the experts, the washing-machine makers think.'
'Well let me show you how Philips tested new BB. We saw that your packet says that new BB contains almost three times more power to drive out stains, and stains are a bugbear to washing-machine owners, so our most critical tests were for stain removal. Can I have that towel please? Now, we stained this with tea three days ago. Now we'll wash half using your previous formula and half in new BB.'
'Equal amounts?'
'And identical conditions. Now let's have a look at the results.'
'Right.'
'Here the previous formula hasn't got all the stains out, but with new BB not a shadow of a stain left, it's completely white.'
'I'd say this means that new BB can wash much whiter.'
'Well we're sure that new BB is the only detergent any woman with a Philips machine should use.'
'What better recommendation? So test new BB in your machine. No other powder, soap or detergent can wash whiter than new energy BB.'

5. (Hand clapping.)
'Now I'm going to put the new Supermatic through its paces. First we add the powder.'
'Why BB?'
'Well Hotpoint know you want the whitest wash you can get and this new energy BB is made to give you extra whiteness even with tough problems, take this terrible blackcurrent stain, for example. Here. (Sounds of tearing.) Take this half and I'll wash this half in new BB. We'll see how white it's

come up? Let's compare it with your half.' (Sounds of people talking.)

'It's marvellous, not a shadow of a stain left. I can tell you my powder wouldn't get it so white.'

'Well now you see why we use the new BB. There isn't another detergent that washes whiter. In fact it is the only detergent we tell Hotpoint owners to use. New energy BB.'

6. (Sounds of birds chirping.)

This is Trenear Estate, Penzance. And this is new energy BB, now with nearly three times more power to remove stains new BB washes much whiter. But we're asking housewives here to test it and only if they're convinced that new BB washes whiter than the powder they've used before to bring proof of that new BB whiteness to this marquee by 10 o'clock tomorrow.

(Sound of clock striking ten.)

'Right. Now let's go inside and see how many more housewives vote that new BB washes whiter.'

(Sound of people talking.)

'What a turnout. Right ladies, let's see what you've brought. Here's proof from all these housewives that new energy BB washed whiter than the powder they'd used before. But test it yourself and see. No other powder, soap or detergent can wash whiter than new energy BB.'

7. 'Use all the stout, then it gets really dirty.'

'Oh what a nasty stain, I wouldn't like to get it out. I don't think I'd ever get it white again.'

'Now, we'll put it in our new Hoover tumble dryer to set it. (Background noise.)

'There we are. How's that for stain?'

'It's revolting, I don't think you could get it clean. I should say it's almost impossible to get it clean.'

'You'd never get that stain out.'

'Now, I'm going to tear it in half and I'm going to give one of you one half and I'm going to put the other half in the washing machine to get it white.'

'What do you use to get it out?'

'We're going to use new energy BB. It's got unbeatable stain removal power. Thank you, Margaret. Now where's my lady with the other half?'

'Here we are.'

'There we are, how's that for whiteness?' (Exclamations.)

'I didn't think it was possible.'

'Now you can see why Hoover recommend new energy BB and no other detergent.'

8. 'Have you bought any washing powder for the family wash day?'

'Yes.'

'What have you bought?'

'BB.'

'BB. Can you tell me why?'

'I have been using BB for many years and I find it's the best.'

'What distinguishes . . . really do?'

'Yes.'

'What sort of washing problems do you have?'

'I have four kids with white school blouses and white school shirts and youngsters get filthy.'

'Do you find that the blue whiteness makes any difference?'

'I would choose it because it's blue because I have the feeling that . . . makes the difference.'

'In that case would you swop your packet of BB? (Background noise.) Would you swop it for that of another leading washing powder?'

'No.' (Laughs.)

'No. Well supposing I give you two. All right two leading washing powders in exchange for your packet of BB.'

'No.'

'You won't swop?'

'No.'

'No other . . . BB users don't swop. But are you that . . . the white wash is your wash? You will be with BB.'

9. 'I see you've bought BB?'

'Yes.'

'Are you really looking forward to your wash with BB?'

'It really brings out the true . . .' (Background noise.)

'Have you tried any of the new powders from the Common Market recently?'

'Well I tried different ones, but I prefer my BB and my husband, my husband is a . . . and is white and I've tried lots of different things with that but I don't think they bring it up as white as what BB does, they come up lovely.'

'Here we have two large packets of other leading powders, you probably recognize them.'

'Yes.'

'Don't look at me like that, it's a very fair offer; we'll do a swop with those for your packet of BB.'

'No. I'll stick to my BB.'

'You'll probably find most BB users won't swop.'

'No not me.'

'You try BB whiteness with . . . you won't swop either.'

10. 'Now why have you bought that?'

'Well I like it . . . and I get a lot of trouble with him.'

'You get a lot of trouble with him, your son?'

'Well he's a rail enthusiast you see . . . cleaning the engines you know . . .'

'They get dirty?'

'He has a steam brush, I have a BB brush.' (Laughs.)

'Anything special about BB whiteness?'

'Well I'll tell you I do think with that blue in you don't need to buy . . . blue now.'

'I've got here two large packets of leading washing powders. Would you swop those two packets for your packet of BB?'

'The only thing I'll swop you is two packets of BB for one.'

'No I can't do that. So you'll stick to it then?'

'Of course.'

'That's what we find, you see most BB users won't swop. Try BB whiteness and I bet you won't swop either.'

11. 'Did you boil that to get it as white as that?'

'No, no, no.'

'You really couldn't have anything whiter than . . .'

'No.'

'And that was in cold water?'

'Yes.'

'How do you think that BB compares?'
'I still prefer BB. A much whiter blue-white.'
'Well anyway there are two large packets and I'm going to take your packet of BB in exchange.'
'No.'
'No?'
'We'll keep the BB.'
'Hang on, only one size. In hot water, even in cool, most BB users won't swop.'

12. 'Here's someone else who's bought new blue BB. Let's see if she's noticed what's new about it.'
(Background noise.)
'What sort of things do you have to wash?'
'Nappies, underwear, shirts, woollies.'
'Yes.'
'Everything.'
'What sort of temperature range do you wash in?'
'Hot, cold, medium.'
'And how do you wash that?'
'Cold water and then drip dry.'
'Would you swop new blue BB?'
'No I'll keep my BB if you don't mind.'
'But you test new blue BB. In hot, even in cool water you get the whitest looking BB wash ever.'

13. 'There's another housewife who's bought new blue BB. Let's see if she's noticed what's new about it.'
'I've noticed it's much lighter.'
'Are you pleased?'
'Yes, particularly I think they're much whiter and I think when you put them on the line you see a big difference.'
'Do you get equally good whiteness in cool water?'
'Yes. I didn't notice . . .'
'Are you wearing anything that's been washed in BB?'
'Oh yes, my dress.'
'You're very pleased?'
'Oh yes.'
'Well let me . . . Look what's in there?'
'Nothing.'

'That's absolutely right. You take it. Now look you can go round the store and fill it with anything you like.'
'No I wouldn't swop my BB. It'll take you a long time to find something like this.'
'Ah well you see she won't swop. But you test it, in hot, even in cool water new blue BB will give you the whitest looking BB wash ever.'

14. 'How long have you been using new blue BB?'
'Ever since . . .'
'Have you noticed any difference in the whiteness that you're getting now?'
'I was satisfied before, but I'm still more satisfied now.'
'What sort of things do you have to wash?'
'My boy he wears white things for football and when you wash it with BB . . .'
'What sort of whiteness do you get in cool water?'
'Just the same. Just as good.'
'Could you describe the sort of whiteness you get?'
'Whiteness that is as good as gold.'
'As good as gold. Thanks very much. Would you swop your packet of new blue BB for anything else?'
'Definitely not.'
'But what am I going to do with this?'
'I don't know, I want to keep my new BB.'
'So I can't give you this . . . But you test it in hot, even in cool water you'll get the whitest looking BB wash ever.'

15. 'What sort of temperature of washing do you do? Hot water? Cold water?
'Both, because sweaters I wash cool and other things I put in the washing machine.'
'What about whiteness in hot water?'
'Marvellous for things like linen and things you put on the table.'
'What about whiteness in cool water?'
'Super. Pants, bras, you name it.'
'Would you swop your packet of new blue BB for anything else?'
'No I wouldn't, I know it's good.'

'Why don't you test new blue BB in hot water, even in cool it will give you the lightest looking BB wash ever.'

16. 'Why did you stop . . .?'

17. 'No, I don't want to swop, I like BB.'
'Why?'
''Cos it always gets clothes very white and things like . . . always come up white and soft as well.'
'They're done in hot water, what about cold water washing?'
'Me jumper's lovely and white.'
'Do you think the blue whiteness has got anything to do with it?'
'Yes, the blue in it makes it look whiter.'
'Am I not going to be able to tempt you to swop your packet?'
'No, I've used both of them and I don't like them. Not as much as I do BB.'
'Why don't you test it yourself? In hot, even in cool water you'll get the whitest looking BB wash ever.'

18. 'And you haven't bought blue BB today?'
'No, I haven't.'
'Are you happy with the powder that you have bought?'
'I am, yes.'
'What sort of things are you looking for?'
'Whiteness and softness.'
'Do you think it could be improved on?'
'I don't think so, no.'
'You could test a packet of new blue BB and tell us what you think about it.'
'Yes, I will test it.'
'Have you done your BB wash?'
'Yes.'
'What's the verdict?'
'Oh, you can see. I mean they're beautiful, white and crisp, but you can notice too the blueness when you have a heap of it.'
'In what sort of temperature range did you wash?'
'In all temperatures in hot wash and orlon nylon.'
'You said your old powder gave you whiteness. I've got two

large packs of your old powder here, would you swop back for those?'

'No, not now.'

'Why not?'

'Because I have had such an improvement with just one wash.'

'Well, perhaps the whiteness of your wash can be improved. Test new blue BB and see in hot, even in cool water you could have the whitest looking BB wash ever.'

Appendix III. Brand R (BR) advertisements

S_1C_1 Sometimes you need a bit of a break—like dinner for two. Something a bit different. That's when I serve BR Beef Curry. A touch of Indian magic. Fluffy rice, tasty beef, oriental fruits and vegetables in real curry sauce. It's a foolproof way to serve something special. Nice to get away from it all.
'Mummy . . .'

S_1C_2 When you've been married a long time—a whole three weeks—you want to find a special way to show how much you love him, something new and special for supper. BR Chop Suey—your first Chinese meal at home—it's got everything, tender beef, the right vegetables in a real sweet and sour sauce with crispy noodles and you did it all. Foolproof BR Chop Suey—get some for your bottom drawer.

S_1C_3 When your own husband starts praising your best friend's cooking, perhaps you should try something different at home—like BR Chicken Curry. Mmmm, tender pieces of chicken, heaps of rice and a curry sauce fit for a prince. It's the foolproof way to serve something special. Why don't you get yourself treated like a princess—with BR Chicken Curry.

S_1C_4 Things were very different the first time I served him BR Beef Curry.
('Remember how we met all those years ago . . .')
He hardly noticed me.

179

('I just looked at you—and I found to my surprise you were looking too . . .')
Then he took a forkful,
('You were here to stay . . .')
and that look said everything.
('Never look away')
And now when he tucks into that fluffy rice and super beef curry he says, 'Mmmm, nice—what is it?'
From BR with love!

S₁C₅ It's funny, but the first time we met we were eating Chow Mein.
('Remember how we met all those years ago . . .')
It was one of those things.
('I just looked at you . . .')
My hair must have looked awful—but he didn't seem to mind.
('. . . your smile said you were here to stay.')
We have BR Chow Mein quite a lot now. Beef, vegetables, and he loves those crispy noodles. He still teases me about the chop sticks. I'll never learn—anyway I'm rather glad.
From BR with love!

S₁C₆ Tonight we had BR Beef Risotto.
('Remember how we met all those years ago . . .')
And I thought about our honeymoon in Venice—it just rained and rained, but we didn't care.
('Your smile said you were here to stay—forever.')
I shall never forget that restaurant. We had risotto with beef and peppers and rice all golden, just like BR do it, and a glass of wine, and super memories.
From BR with love!

S₁C₇ He remembered our anniversary. The least I could do was plan something special for supper. No trouble with BR Chow Mein and good, too. Men like beef, and there's plenty. Soft and crispy noodles and vegetables done the Chinese way, with a touch of soy sauce. It's my foolproof way to serve something special. Mmmm, it looks like I'll need BR Chow Mein again.

S_2C_1 (Singing.)
You don't have to speak the language to know if an Italian's happy or sad.
(Singing.)
With BR Beef Risotto just like Mama used to make, diced beef and rice, with mushrooms, onions, carrots, peas and peppers. The works.
'Bellissimo.'
Get some and enjoy it. BR Beef Risotto. Just like Mama used to make.

S_2C_1 You know you really ought to try BR Beef Risotto—diced beef and vegetables with rice. 'Bellissimo.'
Just like Mama used to make.

S_2C_2 Did you ever see a Chinaman smile? Look in one night when the family's eating BR Chop Suey, just like mother used to make. Lots of good beef and vegetables with rice, topped with deep-fried crispy noodles. Unforgettable! (Laughing.) Try it—BR Chop Suey—and smile!

S_2C_2 Did you ever see a Chinaman smile? Watch him eat BR Chop Suey. Good beef and vegetables with rice, topped with crispy noodles—just like mother used to make. (same copy)

S_2C_3 Beautifully Indian—beautifully Indian—BR Beef Curry with rice. Just like mother used to make. Beautiful curry. Beautiful rice. Beautiful! You should try it. BR Beef Curry with rice—beautifully Indian.

S_2C_3 Beautifully Indian—BR Beef Curry with rice—just like mother used to make. Beautiful curry, beautiful rice. Beautiful! (same copy)

S_3C_1 Enjoy it. BR make their beef curry with the fluffiest rice, the choicest beef, the tastiest curry—and lots of love!

S_3C_2 BR make their chow mein with soft noodles, beef, vegetables, soy sauce, crispy noodles and lots of love!

S_3C_3 Enjoy it. BR make their beef risotto with choice beef, red and green peppers, golden rice and lots of love!

S_3C_4 Enjoy it. BR make their paella with golden rice, the juiciest prawns, chicken, a touch of spice and lots of love!

S_3C_5 Enjoy it. BR make their chicken curry with tender chicken pieces, spiced with sultanas, served with patna rice and lots of love!

S_3C_6 Enjoy it. BR make their chop suey with savoury beef, crispy noodles, fluffy rice, topped with sweet and sour sauce and lots of love!

S_4C_1 This is the mood in which perfect chicken curry is made. BR Chicken Curry captures that mood for you, for him, and that moment made special by BR.

S_4C_2 This is the mood in which perfect beef risotto is made. BR Beef Risotto captures that mood for you, for him, and that moment made special by BR.

S_4C_3 This is the mood in which perfect paella is made. BR Paella captures that mood for you, for him, and that moment made special by BR.

S_4C_4 This is the mood in which perfect chow mein is made. BR Chow Mein captures that mood for you, for him, and that moment made special by BR.

S_4C_5 This is the mood in which perfect beef curry is made. BR Beef Curry captures that mood for you, for him, and that moment made special by BR.

S_4C_6 A new BR? No, a new kind of BR—BR Oven Dishes. Good things come out of the oven and the best are BR. Here's Kentucky Chicken Deep South Casserole—rich and creamy with sweetcorn and red peppers and the fluffiest dumplings that ever came out of an oven. Kentucky Chicken—one of three new oven dishes from BR. Good things come out of an oven and the best are BR.

S_5C_1 BR have found a new twist.
('Figaro . . .')
Now everyone knows what goes to make new BR Beef Italian special. Only BR know how.

S_5C_2 Anyone knows what goes to make the best beef curry. Anyone knows BR know how.

S_5C_3 Anyone knows what goes to make the best beef risotto. Anyone knows BR know how.

S_5C_4 Anyone knows what goes to make the best chow mein. Anyone knows BR know how.

S_5C_5 BR unveils something new—lamb curry. Now everyone knows what goes to make new BR Lamb Curry special. BR know how.

S_5C_6 Anyone knows what goes to make the best beef curry. Anyone knows BR know how.

Appendix IV. Brand E (BE) advertisements

S_1C_1 Mrs Peck was especially fussy about her beans—tossing out stringy ones, skinny ones, rubbery ones, and she got perfect ones for just a few short weeks each year. Until she discovered BE Sliced Green Beans. BE choose only tender perfect beans on the very day they're at their best. So, if they're BE's choice, they must taste good. Now Mrs Peck always chooses BE—and grows flowers in her bean patch.

S_1C_2 The question is—can a vegetable make a good meal memorable? BE think so—take a closer look at what new BE Petit Pois can do. They are BE's new variety of these very special peas—tiny, tender, delicate in flavour. It takes a taste like BE Petit Pois to make good meals memorable— new BE Petit Pois.

S_2C_1 'Sprouts, lady—this time of the year! Sorry, darlin', they're finished. Yes, dear . . .'
('When sprouts are out of season, there's an extra special reason to stop at the BE shop.')
Small young BE Brussel Sprouts. Delicious. Try some!

S_2C_2 'Sprouts. My kids love sprouts, but they're all finished now.'
('When sprouts are out of season, there's an extra special reason to stop at the BE shop.') Small young BE Brussel Sprouts. Delicious. Try some!

S_2C_3 'I'm tired of scraping things off their plates. I say, "roll on the bean season".'
('When beans are out of season, there's an extra special

reason to stop at the BE shop.') Young, tender BE Sliced Green Beans. Delicious. Try some!

S_2C_4 'What, green beans, Mrs—cor, not till the summer.' ('When beans are out of season, there's an extra special reason to stop at the BE shop.') Young, tender BE Sliced Green Beans. Delicious, try some!

S_3C_1 ('BE country. Come home to BE country.') This is where BE Peas come from. They're smaller and they're sweeter and so they should be. ('Come home to BE country—BE country.') For smaller, sweeter peas.

S_3C_1 This is BE country, ('BE country') where BE peas are grown. ('Come home to BE country.') BE peas are chosen smaller for sweeter, more delicate, taste. ('Come home to BE country—BE country.') BE peas are chosen smaller to taste even sweeter. (Different copy)

S_3C_2 ('BE country—Come home to BE country.') Where BE Peas come from. ('BE country.') Chosen smaller to taste even sweeter. BE Peas.

S_3C_3 ('BE country—Come home to BE country.') BE Green Beans, ('BE country') tender young green beans— from BE.

S_3C_4 This is BE country ('BE country'), where BE peas are grown. ('Come home to BE country.') For smaller, sweeter peas. ('BE country') BE peas are chosen smaller to taste even sweeter.

S_3C_5 Seems as if winter will last forever. Day after day the land lies sleeping—but time flies, even in the country, and soon these fields will grow green with a new crop of BE Peas— perfect little peas, small and sweet. ('Come home to BE country. BE country.') For the smallest, sweetest peas in all the land.

S_3C_6 The land lies fallow in BE country—resting, gathering strength for spring. While in a few short months these fields will be full of the goodness of young green beans. BE Green Beans, juicy and tender. ('Come home to BE country—BE country.') For the youngest, tenderest green beans in all the land.

S_3C_6 The land lies fallow in BE country, but in a few short months the fields will be full of young green beans—BE Beans. ('Come home to BE country—BE country.') For the youngest, tenderest green beans in all the land.

S_3C_7 Scarcely a sound spoils the quiet of evening in BE country. One last look to see if these little peas are ready for picking. BE peas—small and sweet. Perfect peas. ('Come home to BE country—BE country.') For the smallest, sweetest peas in all the land.

S_3C_8 Now the mornings are crisp and cold in BE country. Time to bring in the brussels, small and firm, full of taste. ('Come home to BE country—BE country.') For the tastiest brussels in all the land.

S_3C_9 Someone stirs. The sun still sleeps, but in BE country they have no time to lie abed. Soon they will harvest glistening green beans. BE green beans—picked young to taste tender. ('Come home to BE country—BE country.')
For the youngest, tenderest green beans in all the land.

S_3C_{10} There's no time to lie abed in BE country. Soon they will harvest glistening green beans. BE green beans, young and tender. ('Come home to BE country—BE country.')
For the youngest, tenderest green beans in all the land.

S_3C_{11} In BE country we grow things slowly. From the soil springs the shoot, from the shoot the vine, and from the vine the pod that fills with perfect little peas. That's when we pick them, when they're small and sweet. ('Come home to BE country—BE country.') For the smallest, sweetest peas in all the land. BE peas.

S_3C_{11} In BE country we grow things slowly. From the soil springs the vine and from the vine the pod that fills with perfect little peas, and that's when we pick them.
('Come home to BE country—BE country.')
For the smallest, sweetest peas in all the land. BE peas. (Different copy)

S_3C_{11} In BE country we grow things slowly. From the soil springs the shoot, from the shoot the vine and from the vine the pod that fills with perfect little peas. That's when we pick 'em, when they're small and sweet.
('Come home to BE country—BE country.')
For the smallest, sweetest peas in all the land. BE peas. (Different visuals)

S_3C_{11} In BE country we grow things slowly. From the soil springs the shoot, from the shoot the vine and from the vine the pod that fills with perfect little peas. That's when we pick them, when they're small and sweet.
('Come home to BE country—BE country.')
For the smallest, sweetest peas in all the land. BE peas. (Different visuals)

S_3C_{12} When you pick peas, you want to make sure they're the sweetest peas. In BE country we're sure, because we pick them when they're at their youngest. BE country peas. ('Come home to BE country—BE country.') Every one that little bit sweeter, because we pick 'em younger.

S_3C_{12} When you pick peas, you want to make sure they're the sweetest peas. In BE country we're sure, because we pick them when they're at their youngest. BE country peas. ('Come home to BE country—BE country.') Every one that little bit sweeter, because we pick 'em younger. (Different visuals.)

S_3C_{12} When you pick peas, you want to make sure they're the sweetest peas. In BE country we're sure, because we pick them when they're at their youngest. BE country peas. ('Come home to BE country—BE country.') Every one that little bit sweeter, because we pick 'em younger. (Different visuals.)

S_3C_{13} In BE country stand rows of young green beans. BE country beans, the tender ones, picked young—almost before they're grown.

('Come home to BE country—BE country.')

For the youngest, tenderest sliced green beans. BE Beans.

S_3C_{14} Try BE Mixed Vegetables. BE take the sweetest of sweet-corn, the smallest peas, the juiciest carrots, the crispest green beans and mix them together, so BE Mixed Vegetables are the tenderest, tastiest mixed vegetables. Try all that's best from BE country. Try BE Mixed Vegetables.

S_4C_1 Here's tempting value—BE Green Beans, now in handy packs. You cut, you pour, you cook, you store. Get BE Green Beans, now in handy packs at attractive prices.

S_4C_2 Get a taste of real value—BE Brussel Sprouts, now in handy packs—you cut, you pour, you cook, you store. Choose BE Brussel Sprouts now in handy packs at attractive new prices.

S_4C_3 Here's sizzling news from BE—Crinkle Cut Chips, in handy packs. You cut, you pour and what you don't use you store. Get BE Crinkle Cut Chips in handy packs at attractive prices.

S_4C_4 It's the great BE beananza—save 2d, 3d, on the tenderest, tastiest green beans. Save on the great BE beananza—save 2d, 3d, on BE Sliced Green Beans.

S_4C_5 I'm speaking to you from the heart of BE country and this is the new season's crop of BE Peas. It's so good they're putting their money on it. There's 2d off in your shops now.

S_4C_6 Prices are going up and up, but here's something that's going down. BE Sliced Green Beans. Large pack down 3d, $\frac{1}{2}$lb down 2d. BE Sliced Green Beans really down in price.

S_4C_7 A great harvest last year and BE are passing the savings on.

BE Peas are down in price, $\frac{1}{2}$lb down 1d, 1lb down 2d.
Economy size—3d. This must be today's greatest value.

S$_4$C$_8$ 'Hey, did you know—BE are giving away free servings of
beans with a large pack. There you are $\frac{1}{4}$lb free. I'm asking
Fred and Edie round—the extra won't cost me a bean.
(Hello, Fred, is Edie there? . . .)'

S$_4$C$_9$ In BE country the harvest was plentiful, so BE peas are
down in price. Now for the smallest, sweetest peas you pay
a smaller, sweeter price, so buy BE.

S$_5$C$_1$ 'I say, excuse me, madam. Madam have you seen this—BE
peas are down in price. The $\frac{1}{2}$lb down 1d, the 1lb down 2d
and the economy size is down 3d. Look, BE peas are
cheaper.'

S$_5$C$_2$ 'Excuse me, madam . . .'
'Oh look at BE Peas . . .'
'Yes, but madam . . .'
'The 1lb pack down 2d—economy size down 3d. I'll take
one of those.'
'Good idea!'

S$_6$C$_1$ Who says potatoes are ordinary? Not BE!
('New from BE—Potato Fries.')
New BE Potato Fries are round, crinkly slices of potato,
pre-fried by BE to taste extra crisp. There's a great new
potato idea!
('New from BE—Potato Fries.')
Taste that new shape.

S$_6$C$_1$ Who says potatoes are ordinary? Not BE!
('New from BE—Potato Fries.')
New BE Fries are round, crinkly slices of potato, pre-fried
by BE to taste extra crisp. There's a great new potato idea!
('New from BE—Potato Fries.')
Taste that new shape. (Different Copy.)

S$_6$C$_2$ 'What have you got there, John?' 'Potato Fries.'

'You mean fried potatoes.' 'No. Potato Fries—from BE.'
'What are they like?'

'Well, they're rather hard to describe really. They taste
quite like fat crisps. Fat corrugated crisps, but fluffy inside.'
'I see what you mean.' 'Hey, they've definitely got grooves.
In fact, John, they're very groovy potatoes, these BE Potato
Fries. Is that all you're having for your dinner, John?'
'Why not? It might start a trend.'

S_6C_3 'Who'd have thought BE could have done such beautiful
things with a spud as these Potato Fritters.'

'It's the batter.' Shaun thinks it's the batter—'No, it's the
potato.' Paul says it's the potatoes—the lightest, fluffiest
potatoes outside of Ireland. Meself—I think it's the two
together that makes the change—to make Potato Fritters so
fluffy and so crunchy. There must be an Irishman working
at BE!

Bibliography

I. *Books*

Abrams, M. H. *Natural Supernaturalism*. New York: W. W. Norton, 1971.

Allen, J. P. B. and Burenvan, P., eds. *Chomsky: Selected Readings*. Oxford University Press, 1971.

Aron, R. *Main Currents in Sociological Thought*. Vol. 2. Weidenfeld & Nicolson, 1967.

Auzias, J. M. *Chefs pour le structuralisme*. Paris: Seghers, 1967.

Banton, M., ed. *The Relevance of Models for Social Anthropology*. Tavistock Publications, 1965.

———. *The Social Anthropology of Complex Societies*. Tavistock Publications, 1966.

Barthes, R. *Mythologies*. Paris: Editions du Seuil, 1957.

———. *Essais critiques*. Paris: Editions du Seuil, 1964.

———. *Elements of Semiology*. Jonathan Cape, 1967.

———. *Système de la mode*. Paris: Editions du Seuil, 1967.

Bauer, R. A. and Greyser, S. A. *Advertising in America: the Consumer View*. Boston: Harvard University Press, 1968.

Beals, A. R. *Culture in Process*. New York: Holt, Rinehart and Winston, 1967.

Bell, D. *The End of Ideology*. Rev. ed. New York: The Free Press, 1962.

Bendix, R. *Max Weber*. New York: Anchor Books, 1962.

Benedict, R. *Patterns of Culture*. Routledge & Kegan Paul, 1935.

Berger, P. L. *The Social Reality of Religion*. Faber, 1969.

Berger, P. L. and Luckmann, T. *The Social Construction of Reality*. New York: Anchor Books, 1967.

Bernstein, B. *Class, Codes and Control*. Vol. I. Routledge & Kegan Paul, 1971. Vols. II and III. Routledge & Kegan Paul, 1973.

Bliss, P., ed. *Marketing and the Behavioural Sciences*. Boston: Allyn and Bacon, Inc., 1963.

Bolinger, D. *Aspects of Language*. New York: Harcourt, Brace & World, 1968.

Borger, R. and Cioffi, F., eds. *Explanations in the Behavioural Sciences*. Cambridge University Press, 1970.

Boudon, R. *The Uses of Structuralism*. Heinemann, 1971.

Boulding, K. E. *The Image*. Michigan: Ann Arbor, 1956.

Britt, S. H. *The Spenders*. New York: McGraw-Hill, 1960.

Cassirer, E. *Language and Myth*. New York: Dover Publications, 1946.

Chomsky, N. *Language and Mind*. New York: Harcourt, Brace & World, 1968.

Cicourel, A. V. *Method and Measurement in Sociology.* New York: The Free Press, 1964.

Cirlot, J. E. *A Dictionary of Symbols.* Routledge & Kegan Paul, 1962.

Clark, L. H. *Consumer Behaviour.* New York: Harper & Brothers, 1958.

Cohen, P. S. *Modern Social Theory.* Heinemann, 1968.

Cressant, P. *Lévi-Strauss.* Paris: Editions Universitaires, 1970.

Crystal, D. *Linguistics.* Penguin Books, 1971.

Dillistone, F. W., ed. *Myth and Symbol.* SPCK, 1966.

Dixon, R. M. W. *What is Language?* Longmans, 1965.

Doob, L. W. *Propaganda.* New York: Henry Hotte, 1935.

Douglas, J., Field, G. A. and Tarpey, L. X. *Human Behavior in Marketing.* Ohio: Charles E. Merrill Books, 1967.

Douglas, M. *Purity and Danger.* Routledge & Kegan Paul, 1966.

———. *Natural Symbols.* Barrie & Jenkins, 1970.

———, ed. *Witchcraft, Confessions and Accusations.* Tavistock Publications. 1970.

Durkheim, E. *The Elementary Forms of Religious Life.* Allen & Unwin, 1915.

Durkheim, E. and Mauss, M. *Primitive Classifications.* Cohen & West, 1963.

Eliade, M. *Images and Symbols.* Harvill Press, 1952.

———. *The Myth of the Eternal Return.* Routledge & Kegan Paul, 1955.

———. *The Sacred and the Profane.* New York: Harper Torch Books, Harper & Row, 1957.

———. *Myths, Dreams and Mysteries.* New York: Harper Torch Books, Harper & Row, 1957.

———. *Patterns in Comparative Religion.* Sheed and Ward, 1958.

———. *Myth and Reality.* Allen & Unwin, 1964.

———. *Shamanism.* Routledge & Kegan Paul, 1964.

Festinger, L. *A Theory of Cognitive Dissonance.* Tavistock Publications, 1959.

Festinger, L. and Katz, D. *Research Methods in the Behavioral Sciences.* New York: Holt, Rinehart & Winston, 1953.

Firth, R. *Essays on Social Organisation and Values.* The Athlone Press, 1964.

Fishman, J. A., ed. *Readings in the Sociology of Language.* The Hague: Mouton, 1970.

Fodor, J. A. and Katz, J. J., eds. *The Structure of Language.* New Jersey: Prentice-Hall, 1964.

Foucault, U. *The Order of Things.* London: Tavistock Publications, 1970.

Freud, Sigmund. *Totem and Taboo.* Routledge & Kegan Paul, 1958.

———. *The Interpretation of Dreams.* Allen & Unwin, 1954.

———. *Collected Papers.* Vol. IV. The Hogarth Press, 1956.

Fromm, E. *Psychoanalysis and Religion.* New Haven: Yale University Press, 1950.

———. *The Sane Society.* Routledge & Kegan Paul, 1956.

———. *The Revolution of Hope.* New York: Harper & Row, 1968.

Galbraith, J. K. *The Affluent Society.* Hamish Hamilton, 1958.

———. *The Liberal Hour.* Hamish Hamilton, 1960.

———. *The New Industrial State.* Hamish Hamilton, 1967.

Ginsberg, M. *Reason and Unreason in Society.* Vol. II. Heinemann, 1947.

Glansdorff. *Les déterminants de la théorie général de la valeur*. Bruxelles: Université Libre de Bruxelles, 1966.

Goffman, E. *Behaviour in Public Places*. New York: The Free Press, 1963.

———. *The Presentation of Self in Everyday Life*. Allen Lane, The Penguin Press, 1969.

———. *Strategic Interaction*. Oxford, 1970.

Greenberg, J. H., ed. *Universals of Language*, 2nd ed. M.I.T. Press, 1963.

Greenwald, A. G., et al., eds. *Psychological Foundation of Attitudes*. New York: Academic Press, 1968.

Greimas, A. J. *Du sens*. Paris: Editions du seuil, 1970.

Halbwachs, M. *Les cadres sociaux de la mémoire*. Paris: Librairie Felix Alcan, 1925.

———. *La mémoire collective*. 2nd ed. Paris: Presses Universitaires de France, 1968.

Hampden-Turner, C. *Radical Man*. Massachusetts: Schenkman Pub. Co., 1970.

Hayes, E. N. and Hayes, T. *Claude Lévi-Strauss, the Anthropologist as a Hero*. Cambridge, Mass: M.I.T. Press, 1970.

Hjelmslev, L. *Prolegomena to a Theory of Language*. Wisconsin: The University of Wisconsin Press, 1961.

Hilliard, A. L. *The Forms of Value*. New York: Columbia University Press, 1950.

Jung, C. G. *The Interpretation of Nature and the Psyche*. Routledge & Kegan Paul, 1955.

———. *The Archetypes and the Collective Unconscious*. Routledge & Kegan Paul, 1959.

———. *The Structure and Dynamics of the Psyche*. Routledge & Kegan Paul, 1960.

———. *Psychological Reflections*. Routledge & Kegan Paul, 1971.

———. *Memories, Dreams, Reflections*. Fontana, 1971.

———. *Four Archetypes*. Routledge & Kegan Paul, 1972.

Jung, C. G. and Kerenyi, C. *Introduction to the Science of Mythology*. Routledge & Kegan Paul, 1951.

Katona, G. *The Powerful Consumer*. New York: McGraw-Hill, 1960.

———. *The Mass Consumption Society*. New York: McGraw-Hill, 1964.

Katz, J. J. *The Philosophy of Language*. New York: Harper & Row, 1966.

Katz, J. J. and Postal, P. M. *An Integrated Theory of Linguistic Descriptions*. Cambridge, Mass: M.I.T. Press, 1964.

Kitagawa, J. M. and Long, C. H. *Myths and Symbols*. Chicago: The University of Chicago Press, 1969.

Kluckhohn, F. R. and Strodtbeck, F. L. *Variations in Value Orientations*. New York: Raw Peterson, 1961.

Kroeber, A. L. and Kluckhohn, C. *Culture*. New York: Vintage Books, 1952.

Labour Party. *Report of a Commission of Enquiry into Advertising*.

Laing, R. D., Phillipson, H. and Lee, A. R. *Interpersonal Perception*. Tavistock Publications, 1966.

Lane, M., ed. *Structuralism*. Jonathan Cape, 1970.

Lasswell, H. D., Lerner, D. and Sola Pool, de I. *The Comparative Study of Symbols*. Stanford University Press, 1952.

Lazarsfeld, P. F. and Rosenberg, M., eds. *The Language of Social Research*. New York: The Free Press, 1955.

Leach, E. R., ed. *The Structural Study of a Myth*. Tavistock Publications, 1967.

————. *Genesis as Myth*. Cape Editions, 1969.

————. *Lévi-Strauss*. Fontana, 1970.

Lennenberg, E. H., ed. *New Directions in the Study of Language*. Cambridge, Mass: M.I.T. Press, 1964.

Lennenberg, E. H. *Biological Foundations of Language*. New York: John Wiley, 1967.

Lévi-Strauss, C. *The Savage Mind*. Weidenfeld & Nicolson, 1966.

————. *Structural Anthropology*. Allen Lane, The Penguin Press, 1968.

————. *Totemism*. Penguin Books, 1969.

————. *The Elementary Structures of Kinship*. Eyre & Spottiswoode, 1969.

————. *The Raw and the Cooked*. Mythologiques I. Jonathan Cape, 1970.

————. *Du miel aux cendres*. Mythologiques II. Paris: Plon, 1966.

————. *L'origine des manières de table*. Mythologiques III. Paris: Plon, 1968.

————. *L'Homme nu*. Mythologiques IV. Paris: Plon, 1971.

Lyons, J. *Structural Semantics*. Oxford: Basil Blackwell, 1967.

————. *Introduction to Theoretical Linguistics*. Penguin Books, 1968.

————. *Chomsky*. Fontana, 1970.

————, ed. *New Horizons in Linguistics*. Penguin Books, 1970.

Macfarlane, A. *Witchcraft in Tudor and Stuart England*. Routledge & Kegan Paul, 1970.

MacRae, D. G. *Ideology and Society*. Heinemann, 1961.

Malinowski, B. *Magic, Science and Religion*. New York: Doubleday, 1954.

Mannheim, K. *Man and Society*. Routledge & Kegan Paul, 1940.

————. *Essays on Sociology and Social Psychology*. Routledge & Kegan Paul, 1953.

————. *Essays on the Sociology of Culture*. Routledge & Kegan Paul, 1956.

Maranda, P. and Maranda, E. K., eds. *Structural Analysis of Oral Tradition*. Philadelphia: University of Pennsylvania Press, 1971.

Martinet, A. *Elements of General Linguistics*. Faber, 1964.

Maslow, A. H. *Motivation and Personality*. New York: Harper & Row, 1954.

————. *Toward a Psychology of Being*. 2nd ed. van Nostrand, 1968.

Mayer, P., ed. *Socialisation: the Approach from Social Anthropology*. Tavistock Publications, 1970.

Mead, G. H. *Mind, Self and Society*. Chicago: University of Chicago Press, 1934.

Middleton, J. *Myth and Cosmos*. New York: The Natural History Press, 1967.

Miller, J. *McLuhan*. Fontana, 1971.

Millet, L. and d'Ainvelle, M. V. *Le structuralisme*, Psychotheque. Paris: Editions Universitaires, 1970.

Mills, C. W. and Gerth, H. *Character and Social Structure*. Routledge & Kegan Paul, 1954.

————. *From Max Weber*. New York: A Galaxy Book, 1958.

Mills, C. W. *The Sociological Imagination*. New York: Oxford University Press, 1959.

Myrdal, G. *Value in Social Theory*. Routledge & Kegan Paul, 1958.

McClelland, D. C. *The Achieving Society*. van Nostrand, 1961.

McLuhan, M. *The Mechanical Bride*. Routledge & Kegan Paul, 1951.

——. *The Gutenberg Galaxy*. Routledge & Kegan Paul, 1962.

——. *Understanding Media*. New York: McGraw-Hill, 1965.

——. *The Medium is the Message*. New York: Bantam Books, 1967.

——. *From Cliché to Archetype*. New York: Pocket Books, 1971.

Neumann, E. *The Great Mother*. Routledge & Kegan Paul, 1955.

——. *The Archetypal World of Henry Moore*. Routledge & Kegan Paul, 1959.

Nicosia, F. *Consumer Decision Processes*. New Jersey: Prentice-Hall, 1966.

Palmer, F. *Grammar*. Penguin Books, 1971.

Paz, O. *Claude Lévi-Strauss: an Introduction*. Jonathan Cape, 1971.

Piaget, J. *Structuralism*. Routledge & Kegan Paul, 1971.

Ponofsky, E. *Renaissance and Renascences in Western Art*. Stockholm: Almqvist & Wiksell, 1960.

Riesman, D. and Glazer, N. *The Lonely Crowd*. New Haven, Conn: Yale University Press, 1961.

Robey, D. (ed.). *Structuralism; An Introduction*. Oxford: Clarendon Press, 1973.

Rokeach, M. *Beliefs, Attitudes and Values*. San Francisco: Jossey-Bass, 1969.

Rogers, E. M. *Diffusion of Innovation*. New York: The Free Press, 1962.

Rossi, I., ed. *Structuralism in Perspective*. New York: Dutton, 1971.

Saussure, de, F. *Course in General Linguistics*. McGraw-Hill, 1966.

Schneider, L., ed. *Religion, Culture and Society*. New York: John Wiley, 1964.

Sebeok, U. A. *Myth*. Bloomington, Ind: Indiana University Press, 1958.

Shibutani. *Society and Personality*. New Jersey: Prentice-Hall, 1961.

Sigel, I. E. and Hooper, F. H., eds. *Logical Thinking in Children*. New York: Holt, Rinehart & Winston, 1968.

Singh, J. *Great Ideas in Information Theory, Language and Cybernetics*, New York: Dover, 1966.

Smelser, N. J. *Theory of Collective Behaviour*. Routledge & Kegan Paul, 1962.

——. *The Sociology of Economic Life*. New Jersey: Prentice-Hall, 1963.

——, ed. *Readings on Economic Sociology*. New Jersey: Prentice-Hall, 1965.

Sorokin, P. A. *Social and Cultural Mobility*. Illinois: The Free Press of Glencoe, 1959.

Stearn, G. E., ed. *McLuhan Hot and Cool*. Penguin Books, 1968.

Tunstall, J. *The Advertising Man*. Chapman & Hall, 1964.

——. *Media Sociology*. Constable, 1970.

Ullmann, S. *The Principles of Semantics*. Oxford: Basil Blackwell, 1957.

Veblen, T. *The Theory of the Leisure Class*. Allen & Unwin, 1925.

Wahl, F., ed., *Qu'est-ce que le structuralisme?* Paris: Le Sevil, 1968.

Weber, M. *The Protestant Ethic and the Spirit of Capitalism*. Allen & Unwin, 1930.

——. *The Sociology of Religion*. Methuen, 1965.

——. *Economy and Society*. New York: Bedminster Press, 1968.

White, R. W., ed. *The Study of Lives*. New York: Atherton Press, 1963.

Whorf, B. L. *Language, Thought, and Reality.* Cambridge, Mass: M.I.T. Press, 1956.

Wilden, A. *System and Structure; Essays in Communication and Exchange.* London: Tavistock Publications, 1972.

Wilson, A., ed. *Advertising and the Community.* Manchester University Press, 1968.

Wollheim, R. *Freud.* Fontana, 1971.

Wright, J. S. and Warner, D. S. *Advertising.* New York: McGraw-Hill, 1962.

Yale French Studies. *Structuralism.* 36–7, 1966.

Yinger, J. M. *Religion, Society and the Individual.* New York: Macmillan, 1957.

Zunini, G. *Man and his Religion.* Geoffrey Chapman, 1969.

II. *Articles*

Althusser, L. 'Freud and Lacan.' *New Left Review*, vol. 55 (May–June, 1969), pp. 48–65.

Bernstein, B. 'Language in social strata and sectors' in J. A. Fishman, ed., op. cit.

Boone, E. 'The search for the consumer innovator.' *Journal of Business* (April, 1970), pp. 135–40.

Brandon, S. G. F. 'The weighing of the soul' in J. M. Kitagawa, et al., eds, op. cit.

Burridge, K. O. L. 'Lévi-Strauss and myth' in E. Leach, ed. (1967), op. cit., pp. 91–115.

Byrne, D. 'The ubiquitous relationship: attitude similarity and attraction.' *Human Relations*, vol. 24, no. 3 (June, 1971), pp. 201–7.

Chomsky, N. 'The formal nature of language' in E. H. Lennenberg (1967), op. cit., pp. 397–442.

———. 'Problems of explanation in linguistics' in R. Borger and F. Cioffi eds, op. cit., pp. 425–70.

Culler, J. 'The linguistic basis of structuralism', in D. Robey, ed., op. cit., pp. 20–36.

Douglas, M. 'The meaning of myth' in E. Leach, ed. (1967), op. cit., pp. 49–70.

Dumézil, G. 'The three last voyages of Il'ja of Murom' in J. M. Kitagawa et al., eds, op. cit.

Durand, J. 'Rhétoriques et image publicitaire.' *Communications*, no. 15 (1970), pp. 70–95.

Eco, U. 'Sémiologie des message visuels.' *Communications*, no. 15 (1970), pp. 11–51.

———. 'Social life as a sign system', in D. Robey, ed. (1973), op. cit., pp. 57–72.

Eliade, M. 'Les mythes du monde moderne.' *La Nouvelle Nouvelle Revue Française*, vol. 1 (1953), pp. 440–58.

———. 'Prestiges du mythe cosmogonique.' *Diogenes*, no. 23 (1958), pp. 3–17.

BIBLIOGRAPHY

————. 'Survivals and camouflages of myths.' *Diogenes*, no. 41 (1963), pp. 1–25.

————. 'Mythes de combat et de repos dyades et polarites.' *Eranus-Jahrbuch*, vol. 36 (1968), pp. 59–111.

Ellul, J. 'Modern myths.' *Diogenes*, no. 23 (1958), pp. 23–40.

Godelier, M. 'Systèm, structure et contradiction dans "Le Capital" ', in *Les Temps Modernes*, 246. Paris (1966), p. 828.

————. 'The origins of mythical thought.' *New Left Review*, vol. 69 (September–October 1971), pp. 93–112.

Gaboriau, M. 'Structural anthropology and history' in M. Lane, op. cit.

Greimas, A. J. and Rastier, F. 'The interaction of semiotic constraints' in *Yale French Studies*, no. 41 (1968), pp. 86–105.

Hammel, E. A. 'Sexual symbolism in flatware.' *Kroeber Anthropological Society Papers*, no. 37 (Fall, 1967), pp. 23–30.

Hartman, G. 'Structuralism: the Anglo-American adventure' in *Yale French Studies*, *Structuralism* (1966), pp. 148–65.

Isaac, E. 'Myths, cults and livestock breeding.' *Diogenes*, no. 41 (1963), pp. 70–93.

Kellner, H. 'On the sociolinguistic perspective of the communicative situation.' *Social Research*, vol. 37 (1970), pp. 71–87.

Kennedy, R. E. 'The protestant ethic and the parsis' in N. J. Smelser, ed. (1965), op. cit.

Lacan, J. 'The function of speech and language in psychoanalysis', in A. Wilden, *The Language of Self*. Baltimore: Johns Hopkins, 1968, pp. 1–87.

————. 'L'instance de la lettre dans l'inconscient ou la raison depuis Freud' in *Yale French Studies*, *Structuralism*, op. cit., pp. 112–47.

Leach, E. R. 'Anthropological aspect of language: animal categories and verbal abuse' in E. H. Lennenberg, ed. (1964), op. cit.

Leach, E. R. 'Magical hair' in J. Middleton, ed., op. cit., pp. 77–108.

————. 'The legitimacy of Solomon', in E. R. Leach (1969), op. cit., pp. 25–84.

————. 'Brain-twister', in E. N. Hayes and T. Hayes, eds, op. cit., pp. 123–32.

————. 'Structuralism in social anthropology', in D. Robey, ed. (1973), op. cit., pp. 37–56.

Lennenberg, E. H. 'A biological perspective of language' in E. H. Lennenberg, ed. (1964), op. cit.

————. 'The capacity for language acquisition' in J. A. Fodor and J. J. Katz, eds, op. cit., pp. 579–603.

Lévi-Strauss, C. 'Four Winnebago myths: a structural sketch' in S. Diamons, ed., *Culture in History*. New York: Columbia University Press, 1960, pp. 351–62.

————. La structure et la forme', Cahiers de l'Institute de Science Économique Appliquée, 99, pp. 3–36.

————. 'The story of asdiwal' in E. R. Leach, ed. (1967), op. cit., pp. 1–48.

————. 'A confrontation.' *New Left Review*, vol. 62 (July–August, 1970), pp. 57–74.

Lewis, P. E. 'Merleau-Ponty and the phenomenology of language' in Yale French Studies, *Structuralism*, op. cit., pp. 19–40.

Lyons, J. 'Structuralism and Linguistics' in D. Robey, ed. (1973), op. cit., pp. 5–19.

Macarte, P. 'A new approach in advertising research.' *Advertising Quarterly* (Spring 1970), pp. 36–43.

MacRae, D. G. 'Advertising and social structure.' *Advertising Quarterly*, vol. 1, no. 1 (August, 1964).

———. Introduction to R. Boudon, op. cit.

———. 'The elite and the conspiracy.' *Encounter*, vol. XXXVIII, no. 3 (March, 1972), pp. 75–80.

Maranda, P. 'The computer and the analysis of myths.' *International Social Science Journal*, vol. XXIII, No. 2 (1971), pp. 228–335.

Martinet, A. 'Structure and language' in Yale French Studies, *Structuralism*, op. cit., pp. 10–18.

Maybury-Lewis, D. 'Science or bricolage' in E. N. Hayes and T. Hayes, eds, op. cit., pp. 150–63.

Metz, C. 'Propositions méthodologiques pour l'analyse du film.' *Information sur les Sciences Sociales*, vol. VII, no. 4 (August, 1968), pp. 107–19.

Mills, C. W. 'The cultural apparatus' in I. L. Horowitz, ed., *Power, Politics and People*, the Collected Essays of C. Wright Mills. Oxford University Press, 1963, pp. 405–22.

———. 'Language, logic and culture.' Ibid., pp. 423–38.

———. 'Mass media and public opinion.' Ibid., pp. 577–98.

Müller, 'The "passivity" of language and the experience of nature', in J. M. Kitagawa and C. H. Long, eds, op. cit.

Nutini, H. G. 'Some considerations on the nature of social structure and model building: a critique of Claude Lévi-Strauss and Edmund Leach', in E. N. Hayes and T. Hayes, eds, op. cit., pp. 70–107.

Péninou, G. 'Physique et métaphysique de l'image publicitaire'. *Communications*, no. 15 (1970), pp. 96–109.

Ricoeur, P. 'The problem of the double sense as hermeneutic problem and a semantic problem' in J. M. Kitagawa and C. H. Long, eds, op. cit.

Robertson, T. S. and Kennedy, J. N. 'Predictions of consumer innovators: applications of multiple discriminant analysis'. *Journal of Market Research* (February, 1968), pp. 64–9.

Runciman, W. G. 'What is structuralism?' *British Journal of Sociology*, vol. 20, (1969), pp. 253–65.

Schneider, D. M. 'Some muddles in the models: or, how the system really works' in M. Banton, ed. (1965), op. cit., pp. 25–86.

Sebeok, T. A. 'Coding in the evolution of signalling behaviour', *Behavioural Science*, 7, pp. 430–442.

———. 'Communication in animals and in men: three reviews', in Fishman, ed. (1968), pp. 14–37.

Sorokin, P. A. 'The active ideational culture mentality' in L. Schneider, ed., op. cit.

Steiner, G. 'A conversation with Claude Lévi-Strauss.' *Encounter*, no. 4 (April, 1966), pp. 32–8.

————. 'Orpheus with his myths' in E. N. Hayes and T. Hayes, eds, op. cit., pp. 170–83.

Sutherland, N. S. 'Is the brain a physical system?' in R. Borger and F. Cioffi, eds, op. cit., pp. 97–138.

Yalman, N. ' "The raw : the cooked :: nature : culture"—observations on Le Cru et le cuit' in E. R. Leach, ed. (1967), op. cit., pp. 71–90.

Zimmerman, R. L. 'Lévi-Strauss and the Primitive' in E. N. Hayes and T. Hayes, eds, op. cit., pp. 216–34.

Subject Index

Advertising
    analysis by principles of structuralism, 21–31; application of set theory in study of, 24, 40; as locus of communication, viii, 124–6, 155; as mediator: between abstract and concrete, 34–40, 62–6, 124, 155, between consumer and producer, 124, 155; between social values and consumer behaviour, 122–4, 155; as multi-layer construct, 135–7; as only changing variable in market mix, 99–100; as transformation process, 18; concept of, as myth, ix–x, 153–7; evaluation of efficacy, 134–7; expenditure on, as independent variable in evaluation of impact, 109–18; inter-relation between medium, content, recipient, in impact of, 60, 123–4; nature of binary opposition in, 153–4; need for recurrence to penetrate perceptual barriers, 40, 43; obstacles to be overcome on surface, structural levels, 126–7; of brands, products, distinguished, viii–ix, 119–22, 128–34, 137; potential basis for generation of, 157; public rejection of, 34, 123; spill-over effects, 118; static, dynamic distinguished, viii, 24–5, 59–67, 128–9; sub-systems and whole systems distinguished, viii, 139; system effects, 118; total universe of, 40–1; *see also under individual types of product*

Anonymous street interview, function in dynamic advertising, 72–3, 73–4

Antonyms, binary oppositions based on, 28

Anxiety, comparative roles of advertising, myth, in reduction of, 156

Archetypes and the Collective Unconscious, The, Jung, 152–3

Associative relations in static advertising, 38–9

Auditory sign system, inter-relation with other sign systems in dynamic advertising, 59–62

Axioms in structuralist analysis, inter-relation with other elements, 22–4

Baby foods
    structural analysis of advertising campaigns, 24–5, 47–50, 134; targets of advertising, 120, 121

Background, spatial relation with product, in static advertising, 37–40

'Bandwagon' effects, defined, 122–3

Binary oppositions, relations
    classification, types of, 7–8, 28–30; concept of, in linguistic theory, 3–8; existence of redundancies between, 141, 148; fundamental nature of, in advertising, 153–4; human behaviour rooted in, 10–12, 23; identification

War
  concept of, as mediator between various dimensions of ECDs, 145–6;
  concept of binary opposition to peace in various advertising campaigns,
  41–7, 141–9
Washing powders, advertising of
  characteristics, 68–75, 133–4, 160–8, 169–78; public reaction to, 74;
  structural analysis of, 68–75; targets, 120, 121
Woman, choice of data for anlaysis from, 40
Woman's Own, choice of data for analysis from, 40

Index compiled by Brenda Hall, a member of the Society of Indexers.

Author Index